From Christ to Constantine

Jerusalem: centre of the earliest church. The photograph shows the old city and Temple area, now occupied by the Dome of the Rock. In the bottom left-hand corner is the Wailing Wall, the only remaining part of Herod's Temple, destroyed by the Romans in AD 70.

M. A. SMITH

From Christ
to Constantine

Inter-Varsity Press

© INTER-VARSITY PRESS, LONDON
Inter-Varsity Fellowship,
39 Bedford Square, London WC1B 3EY

INTER-VARSITY PRESS
Box F, Downers Grove,
Illinois 60515

First published November 1971

INTERNATIONAL STANDARD BOOK NUMBERS:

UK EDITIONS
Casebound 0 85110 619 6
Paperback 0 85110 570 X

USA EDITION: 0 87784 758 4
Library of Congress catalog card
number : 70-169005

Printed in Great Britain by Billing & Sons Limited,
Guildford & London.

Contents

Illustrations

Time chart

The right-hand column shows the main people and events in the history of the church; the left-hand column gives a list of Roman emperors and some of the events in Roman/Jewish history.

AD

30 Crucifixion and resurrection of Jesus Christ

37–41 Caligula emperor
41–54 Claudius emperor

Jews expelled from Rome
c. 51 Paul at Corinth

54–68 Nero emperor
   64 Great fire at Rome
      Petronius writes

62 Death of James the Lord's brother

c. 66 Death of Peter and Paul
66 Great Jewish revolt begins

69 Year of the four emperors (civil war)

69–79 Vespasian emperor
   70 Destruction of Jerusalem
   72 Last stand of Zealots at Masada

79–81 Titus emperor
   79 Eruption of Vesuvius

81–96 Domitian emperor
96–98 Nerva emperor

c. 95 John exiled to Patmos
c. 96 *1 Clement*

98–117 Trajan emperor
      Tacitus writes
      Juvenal writes

(?) Papias   (?) *Didache*
c. 110 Ignatius goes to Rome
c. 112 Pliny in Bithynia

Rylands fragment of John
Polycarp's letter

117–138 Hadrian emperor
   135 Revolt of Bar Cochba

Barnabas, (?) *2 Clement*, Hermas
c. 136 Valentinus comes to Rome
Quadratus's apology
(?) *Letter to Diognetus*

Justin's dialogue with Trypho

138–161 Antoninus Pius **emperor**	*c.* 140 Marcion at Rome Valentinus's *Gospel of Truth* Basilides
Apuleius writes	Aristides's *Apology* (?) *c.* 156 Martyrdom of Polycarp
Fronto writes	*c.* 160 Beginnings of Montanism
161–180 Marcus Aurelius **emperor**	*c.* 165 Death of Justin Martyr Tatian and the *Diatessaron* Athenagoras, Melito
Lucian of Samosata Celsus' *True Account*	177 Persecution at Lyons Irenaeus goes to France
	179 Conversion of Bardaisan Dionysius of Corinth 180 Martyrs of Scilli
180–192 Commodus emperor	Theophilus of Antioch's Apology Palut bishop of Edessa *c.* 190 Easter controversy Serapion at Rhossus; Pantaenus at Alexandria Rise of Callistus (Marcia's intercession) Clement of Alexandria
193–211 Septimius Severus **emperor**	*c.* 197 Tertullian converted *c.* 200 Chester Beatty papyrus of Paul's letters 202 Martyrdom of Perpetua and Felicitas Martyrdom of Leonides (Origen's father) Clement of Alexandria flees to Cappadocia Noetus comes to Rome (Patripassian controversy) Origen teaching in Alexandria
211–235 Later Severan **dynasty**	Callistus bishop Hippolytus separates
212 Citizenship for all free men in Empire.	*c.* 215 Tertullian joins Montanists *c.* 230 Origen ordained, goes to Syria
235–238 Maximinus Thrax **emperor**	Persecution. Death of Hippolytus
238–244 Gordian III emperor	Origen's *Conversation with Heraclides* Beginnings of Manicheism
244–249 Philip the Arabian **emperor**	Cyprian bishop of Carthage Dionysius bishop of Alexandria
249–251 Decius emperor	Empire-wide persecution

253–260 Valerian emperor	Death of Origen
Gallienus co-emperor	Disputes over lapsed Christians
	Novatian *v*. Cornelius at Rome
	254 Stephen bishop of Rome
256 Destruction of Dura-	
Europos	258 Martyrdom of Cyprian
260–268 Gallienus emperor	Toleration edict
(**Valerian captured**	Clash between the two Dionysii
by Persians)	(?) Minucius Felix
'Thirty Tyrants'	Paul of Samosata bishop of Antioch
Postumus emperor in	
France	*c*. 268 Condemnation of Paul of Samosata
	Death of Dionysius of Alexandria
268–270 Claudius Gothicus	
emperor	
Defeat of the Goths	
270–275 Aurelian emperor	
272 Defeat of Zenobia	274 Eviction of Paul of Samosata
275–276 Tacitus emperor	
276–282 Probus emperor	
285–305 Diocletian and	
Maximian emperors	
	c. 290 Lucian of Antioch
	Lactantius writes
c. 295 Manichees persecuted	
296 British revolt ends	
	303 Start of persecution (search at Cirta)
	305 Empire-wide persecution (church at
	Nicomedia wrecked)
305–311 The later tetrarchy	*c*. 305 Conversion of Arnobius
(**Diocletian and**	
Maximian abdicate)	
306 Death of Constantius	Licinius halts persecution
	Maximin renews persecution
	Melitius
	Martyrdom of Peter of Alexandria and Lucian
	of Antioch
311 Death of Galerius	311 Start of Donatist schism
312–337 Constantine	
emperor (with	
Licinius until 325)	Eusebius of Caesarea writes
312 Battle of Milvian	
Bridge	
313 Defeat of Maximin	313 'Edict of Milan'

Introduction

Church history is not generally popular today. People constantly claim that past centuries are vastly different from our own and so can have no possible relevance to us. But they are wrong: many of our present problems have arisen in other forms before, and it is often most instructive to see how they were faced by Christians of other ages.

The currently modish Eastern mysticism is not new: Christians of the second century AD had to contend with a similar challenge. Debates over Christ and His relation to God the Father were just as common in the early centuries as they are today. People could arrive at answers similar to those given, for example, by the Jehovah's Witnesses, and they needed refutation then as now. There was at least one outbreak of a kind of disruptive Pentecostalism; and when people came claiming to be inspired by the Holy Spirit, the churches had to find reliable means of testing their claims. The current 'science' was often invoked by opponents of Christianity to refute the basic Christian beliefs. And Christians had to decide what was their attitude to the state; they had to distinguish between its just claims, and where it had to be resisted on the grounds of conscience. We may not agree with all their answers to these and other problems, but they are certainly well worth a hearing.

Too often, however, the only church history many Christians know ends with the death of the apostle John in about AD 100 and resumes with Martin Luther and the Reformation in AD 1517. They do not realize that the intervening period, so often glossed over as a time of unrelieved darkness, is in fact highly important for our understanding of Christianity today.

Of this period, the time from the death of the apostles until the official toleration and establishment of Christianity in the last years of the Roman Empire is of vital importance. Full-blown mediaeval Catholicism did not arise overnight. When the apostles died, the cause of Christ was handed on to largely obscure people, who were left with the task of carrying on the work of the apostolic period. Often we have more gaps in our story than concrete facts. Many stories come in versions so distorted that it is hard to decide whether the principal characters were worthy successors to the apostles, or the devil's own agents. Perhaps their contemporaries were as uncertain as we are. But in spite of problems, some sort of coherent narrative can be written. And it repays study, if for no better reason than to warn future followers of Christ to avoid the same errors as their predecessors.

It would be unfair, however, to paint a picture of second-rate men and women muddling on, of interest only as a terrible warning of what not to do. There is much more to the early church than this. The supreme courage shown by the first Christians in just carrying on in spite of opposition compels our admiration; their achievements in the face of fantastic odds astonish us. And they took place without the education, technical skills and church organization which nowadays we take for granted. Lesser people, lacking God's Spirit, must have failed dismally; yet the evidence is that these early Christians struggled on and often succeeded.

By its very nature, this book can be only an introduction. For those who want more detailed information, there are the larger histories where theories are weighed and evidence sifted. Since new material is continually being found and old material is constantly being subjected to reappraisal, the details of the picture are often being slightly altered. But the main thread of the story remains fairly constant. It is also helpful to read what the original authors had to say; many of them are available in English translation.

The greatest justification for studying any history, whether sacred or secular, is that it is the study of people. While the furniture of history changes, the basic human beings do not.

14

Christians are still under the same pressures, and still have the same variety of characters as did their predecessors in the years of the early church. The New Testament states that what happened in ancient times was 'written for our instruction'. It is my conviction that what happened in the early church is not only full of human interest, but is similarly instructive for us today.

1

Handover

Few people ask what happened to the first Christians when the New Testament period ended. In actual fact, their life went on very much as before, except that some of the greatest names were no longer there. So what did happen? There is no single date when the New Testament ends and the post-apostolic period begins. Luke's account of the early church, as given in the Acts of the Apostles, ends in the early 60s, but we have scraps of information up to the end of the first century from the New Testament itself. In the New Testament we see the first signs of movements which were to be of considerable significance in the life of the early church.

Jews and Christians

The most significant fact of the first century from a Christian point of view was the severance of Christianity from Judaism. We often forget that Christianity arose out of Judaism. Jesus Himself was a Jew, although by the standards of His day He was extremely unconventional. While showing complete acceptance of the written Old Testament, He rejected the traditional interpretations as popularized by the Pharisees (especially where these effectively contradicted the commands of the Old Testament law). He condemned, for example, the legal fiction which was used to excuse people from supporting their parents, and He sat light to sabbath regulations when they hindered acts of mercy.[1]

Early on, Christ's followers had to face the problem of how far the new revelation in Jesus Christ could continue within

[1] See Mark 7:9–13; Luke 14:1–6.

Relief from the Arch of Titus, showing Roman soldiers carrying spoils from the Jewish Wars of AD 66–70. The relief is from the passageway of the arch.

the framework of Judaism. The attitudes taken varied. Some, a small minority, wanted Christianity to remain a Jewish sect. Many of the first disciples, Jews themselves, wanted an accommodation for Gentiles, but could not decide how far to relax their rules. How far would it be right, they wondered, to alter the law of God?[2] Paul, and those like him, wanted to cut through the problem. Religiously, Jew and Gentile were to be one in Christ, while leaving the Jew to carry on observing his own particular ethnic customs.[3]

In the event, the battle between Jewish Christians and Gentile Christians was never joined, in spite of some skirmishes such as that recorded in the Epistle to the Galatians. The great Jewish revolt of AD 66, with the subsequent destruction of the Jerusalem Temple in AD 70 by the armies of the emperor Titus, put Jew and Christian on opposite sides.[4] The Christians who still remained in Jerusalem when the revolt broke out came under heavy pressures from the Jewish nationalists. So they left the doomed city and resettled in

[2] See Acts 10:9–11:18; 15:1–11.

[3] See Romans 10:12;1 Corinthians 7:18, 19; Galatians 2:7; 3:28. Even Paul, though a strong advocate of Gentile freedom, as a Jew himself kept Jewish religious customs scrupulously; see, *e.g.*, Acts 21:20–26.

[4] The full account is in Josephus, *Jewish War* ii. 17–vi. 10.

Pella, a town in Transjordan.[5] The Jews put curses on the Nazarenes in their Benedictions (the Synagogue Prayers) shortly after this.[6] The great divide between Jew and Christian was no longer able to be bridged; the future strength of the Christians was to be among Gentiles. Although there continued to be Jewish Christians for some considerable time, they became a tiny minority, often viewed with mistrust on account of their strange practices and beliefs.

But the Jewish revolt of AD 66–70 had other repercussions as well. The dispersal of the Jerusalem church left Christians without a centre of gravity. In retrospect, perhaps this was no great disadvantage. Up till the time just before the revolt, James the Lord's brother had held a position of honour and some influence. He had been the acknowledged leader of the Jerusalem church, and there might have been difficulties if there had ever been the need to appoint a successor. But while one Roman governor was dead and his successor had not arrived from Rome, James's enemies took the law into their

[5] Eusebius, *Church History* iii. 5. 4.
[6] Benediction 12. See C. K. Barrett, *The New Testament Background: Selected Documents* (SPCK, 1957), pp. 166–167.

The Arch of Titus, Rome, erected *c.* AD 81. The Roman victory over the Jews is one of the scenes depicted in relief on the arch.

own hands. James was seized, and after a perfunctory trial was stoned to death.[7]

Nameless missionaries

In the subsequent unsettled period there was no question of the Jerusalem church continuing to exercise its authority. In any case, it had merely a vague primacy of honour, and it is highly unlikely that other congregations would have tolerated any high-handed interference. But the question never arose. After AD 70 the Jerusalem church was effectively out of the picture. But with the end of Luke's narrative in Acts, there is very little left in the way of a picture at all.

Later ages, up to our own, have speculated on what happened next. Perhaps it is better to review the situation as Paul sat in prison. As a result of his missionary work, he had left scattered congregations in Asia Minor and Greece. We know that they were not static: Laodicaea, Hierapolis and Colossae received the gospel from Ephesus.[8] Someone had been to Crete before Titus went there.[9] From the letters to the churches in Revelation we can see evidence of other nameless missionaries.[1]

But this was only part of the story. From 1 Peter we gain the impression of many small groups of believers in parts of Asia Minor unvisited by Paul.[2] We would very much like to know how Apollos[3] first heard of Jesus in Alexandria (through Jewish Christian in the big Jewish quarter there?), and how Priscilla and Aquila[4] were converted before they left Rome. Scholars have noted the similarities between the speech of Stephen in Acts 7 and the Epistle to the Hebrews. This might indicate that some of Stephen's disciples were active among

[7] This happened in AD 62. The account given by Hegesippus is preserved in Eusebius, *Church History* ii. 23. A shorter account is found in Josephus, *Antiquities* xx. 9. 1.

[8] Colossians 1:7; 4:12–16.

[9] Titus 1:5.

[1] Revelation 2 and 3 (churches at Smyrna, Philadelphia and Sardis).

[2] 1 Peter 1:1, 2.

[3] Acts 18:24 ff.

[4] Acts 18:1, 2.

[5] See Hebrews 13:24. 'Those who come from Italy' could be either the senders in Italy or expatriate Italians sending greetings back home.

Map 1

The Eastern Mediterranean Area

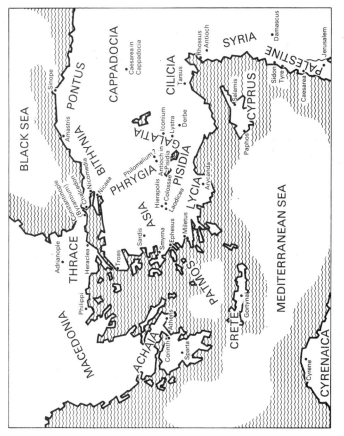

people with some contact with Italy.[5] From a very early period there were Christians as far afield as Cyrene.[6]

Our knowledge of what went on eastwards of Jerusalem is a total blank, but one can hardly imagine that Ananias of Damascus,[7] Paul's first Christian friend, just sat back and did nothing! Antioch was flourishing, and continued to do so (early in the next century one of its leading members, Ignatius, was thought sufficiently important to be taken to feed the lions in the Colosseum at Rome). Amid this scene of largely un-chronicled expansion (we do not even know for certain what was Paul's eventual fate),[8] it seems that the centre of influence moved to the coastal cities of Asia Minor, where the apostle John seems to have settled as father-in-God to the little congregations.

Papias

One of the people who certainly met John was Papias, a church elder of Hierapolis, a small town near Colossae, fifty miles inland from Ephesus in Asia Minor. Because of his tendency to take the book of Revelation too literally, Eusebius (the early fourth-century historian) brands him as of small intelligence.[9] We have little enough of his work to form a judgment of our own. Papias was in the position to question people who had known the twelve apostles, and he records fragments of information about the Gospels. Scholars would give a great deal to have his complete works, since they come down from a period of which we know little, and the fragments that remain (they survive as quotations in the works of later authors) show him to have been in a position to give valuable information. No-one knows now what Papias meant when he says that Matthew wrote his Gospel, or part of it, in Hebrew. He also records that Mark got much of his information from Peter. There has been much debate over whether Papias refers to a John the elder, as distinct from John the apostle.

[6] Acts 11:20. Was Simon of Cyrene the first missionary here?
[7] Acts 9:10 ff.
[8] See the evidence from *1 Clement* (below, p. 26; also the letter of Dionysius of Corinth to Soter, bishop of Rome, in Eusebius, *Church History* ii. 25. 2).
[9] Eusebius, *Church History* iii. 39, where the most important fragments are quoted.

But John the elder is at best a very tenuous figure. It seems more likely that it was the aged apostle who was referred to as 'the old man' (a term of endearment or respect or exasperation? Or perhaps all three!)

To judge from 3 John, the aged apostle did not have everything his own way, even among the congregations of Asia Minor. There were strong characters among the little groups of Christians—people like Diotrephes—and independency seems to have flourished. But internal strife was not the greatest trouble that the little Christian groups had to face. They lived in the world of the Roman Empire. Before long officialdom would notice them. How would Christians be viewed by the Roman government?

The first persecutions

The attitude of the Roman Empire to things religious was equivocal. Provided that you avoided doing anything too outrageous, and provided that you behaved circumspectly towards the 'powers that be', things could be tolerable. The Jews, as a peculiar people in more senses than one, enjoyed a certain amount of favour. But they could not presume on too much, as the sharp letter of the emperor Claudius to the people of Alexandria shows.[1] Christians were at first treated as a kind of Jew. Gallio, who was governor of Greece while Paul was at Corinth, had refused to judge complaints against them.[2] He treated such charges as questions of Jewish religious law, which he had neither the desire nor the competence to unravel. Other provincial governors had taken similar action.

But there were changes in the air. The worship of the emperor was becoming popular.[3] This had originated in the East, where for a long time it had been customary to offer divine honours to any ruler. The conquering Romans had basked in this flattery, and the emperors were beginning to demand the worship which was so often lavished on them.

[1] It survives as Papyrus London 1912. Translated in C. K. Barrett, *The New Testament Background*, pp. 44–47. This took place in AD 41.
[2] Acts 18:12–17. Date about AD 51.
[3] See further p. 75.

With this came a tendency to judge loyalty by the willingness to worship the emperor.

Then came the affair of Nero and the fire at Rome.[4] We shall probably never know why it was the Christians whom Nero decided to use as scapegoats for the fire. It has been suggested that it was the Jewish advisers of his wife Poppaea who encouraged him, but there is little evidence for this. It has also been argued that no law against Christians was ever put on the statute-book, though some later Christian writers seem to think there was a law proscribing Christians by name.[5] Probably it did not matter much.

The Christians were tortured and burned in Nero's gardens in Rome with a savagery that made even unsympathetic observers like the historian Tacitus feel disgust at the emperor's actions. Whether there were similar persecutions in the provinces is not certain. Some scholars think that the change of tone in the last chapters of 1 Peter indicate that this letter was being written at the time when hostility towards Christians was being made official policy. After Nero's death in AD 68, the ensuing Flavian dynasty had no love for the Christians; there is reference to persecution in three of the letters to the churches in the book of Revelation. And it could go as far as the death penalty. Certainly, by the early years of the next century Pliny, the governor of Bithynia (north-west Asia Minor), was in no doubt that Christians should be executed. He only wanted to know on what charge.[6]

[4] AD 64. Main account in Tacitus, *Annals* xv. 44.
[5] Tertullian believed there was such a law. See also Suetonius, *Life of Nero* 16, where persecution of Christians is mentioned among various miscellaneous edicts.
[6] See further below, p. 45.

Coins of four Roman emperors. (1) **Claudius.** (2) **Nero.** (3) **Vespasian.** A special coin to commemorate the capture of Judaea and Jeruslaem in the Jewish Wars. On the reverse are the words 'Judaea capta'; the palm-tree is a symbol of Judaea. (4) **Domitian.** All in the British Museum, London.

1   2

Christians were certainly widespread in Asia Minor, and so targets for persecution, especially during the reign of Domitian. There were rumours that Christians were being persecuted even in the royal household. Certainly, some people in high places whose lives were blameless were executed or banished on the charge of 'atheism'.[7] (A Christian, refusing to pay reverence to the traditional gods of Rome, would seem an 'atheist' to his Roman contemporaries.) It was in such times that the apostle John had a spell in exile on Patmos island (about AD 95),[8] and his vision is recorded in the book of Revelation. The cryptic language of parts of it leaves details uncertain, but persecution by a reincarnation of Nero seems to have been expected. Indeed, persecution may actually have begun. The Christians stood firm and awaited the storm which might bring the last days with it. Then Domitian, the emperor, was removed by a palace revolution (AD 96), and the new emperor reversed his policy. The churches could breathe again, but for how long?

'1 Clement'

Persecution sometimes makes Christians draw closer together. But not always, and certainly not at Corinth. The factions there which had exasperated Paul had continued. A younger group had deposed the older officials, and general anarchy was reigning. It was just after the time of persecution in the late 90s. Somehow the situation became known to the congregation at Rome, and a letter was sent to Corinth. This letter is usually

[7] Dio Cassius, *Epitome* lxvii. 14.
[8] See Revelation 1:9.

3   **4**

attributed to bishop Clement of Rome, but in fact it is an open letter from one church to another. The main subject is, naturally, Christian behaviour. Appeal is made to older examples, such as the patience of Peter and Paul in their sufferings (tantalizing references which unfortunately tell us very little), and the young revolutionaries are told to climb down and reinstate the deposed officials.

Messengers were sent with the letter, to ensure that it was heeded, but we do not know with what result. Once more darkness descends. Some would see this letter as the first step in the rise of the Roman primacy, whereby the bishop of Rome became the leader of Western Christendom. Such a view is exceedingly anachronistic.[9] It was a whole congregation, not one outstanding individual, which was trying to settle troubles in another church. Certainly there was no right invoked other than the universal right of one Christian to admonish another from the Scriptures. Whether Corinth continued to squabble we do not know. Certainly Rome was soon to have its own problems, and perhaps had neither time nor inclination to intervene. As with much else, we just do not know.

The letter from Rome to Corinth also gives an interesting sidelight on the average theology of the church of this period. Appeal for authoritative directions is made to the Synoptic Gospels, Paul's letters and perhaps Hebrews, in addition to copious quotations from the Old Testament. Salvation is seen to be based on faith and works; for example, Rahab is said to have been saved by 'faith and hospitality'. Perhaps the particular situation called for emphasis on faith being accompanied by suitable actions, but it does seem that Paul's doctrine of salvation through the grace of God alone was not well understood.

Early heresies

The early churches were subject to three main problems. We have seen two, namely state persecution and internal strife. The third, and most insidious, was heresy. Upon these tiny Christian minorities in a pagan environment, ideological

[9] On this question, see further below, pp. 92ff.

pressures must have been heavy. The temptation to accommodate to contemporary 'science' or to the latest philosophical fad was always there. In a movement drawn mainly from the less-educated classes, the danger was all the greater. The most articulate leaders and the intellectual élite would be most exposed to these influences and could easily lead an uninstructed and undiscriminating audience astray. The then fashionable Oriental mysticism, the direct challenge of Judaism, and the more earthy pressures to condone lax morality, were ever present.

By and large, the problem of lax morality was the least of the Christians' problems, though there were some notable lapses. Later on, the problem of those who had given in under persecution was to divide some churches. When compared with the then current non-Christian morality, however, the Christians were a shining example.

But there was plenty of temptation to depart from the 'faith once delivered to the saints'. Already in Paul's time there had been an attempt to introduce a heavenly hierarchy alongside Jesus at Colossae.[1] Pressures from a Judaistic legalism were felt in many places[2] (was this due to a mistaken belief that the whole Old Testament was to be followed to the letter?).

More serious was the heresy which the old apostle John had to face, which led people to deny that Jesus was a real human being.[3] Some believed Him to be merely a spirit-being, who had no lasting connection with this material world. While the apostles and their friends survived (people who had actually met Jesus while alive), such wild ideas were refutable. In the next generation it was not going to be so easy.

So the century of Christ and the apostles passed. Their successors were left with the task of carrying on what they had received. They were scattered in little groups, probably meeting in homes, and drawn mainly from the lower social strata. They had their Scriptures: primarily the Old Testament, but this was supplemented by the Gospel accounts of Jesus and the writings of His apostles. They lived under a

[1] Colossians 2:8, 18.
[2] See Galatians, *passim*.
[3] 1 John 2:22; 4:1–6; 2 John 7.

Life in the early Roman Empire. (1) A typical street in **Pompeii,** preserved by the eruption of Vesuvius in 79. Originally the house would have risen to several storeys above street level. (2) Every street corner in **Herculaneum** (destroyed at the same time as Pompeii) had its 'bar'; wine was served from the jars in the 'counter'.

shadow of potential persecution, not knowing exactly where it would break. But they had something which they could pass on. Their knowledge of Christ might seem to us legalistic in emphasis, but in the world of Petronius and Juvenal[4] this was their greatest glory. The seedy world of South Italy which Petronius describes, the corrupt society of imperial Rome which Juvenal castigates, were to face a sudden challenge. The difference between Juvenal who bemoaned decadence, and the Christian who lived it down was just this—that in Christ the Christian had the power and drive to act where others despaired.

The handover had been completed. By events largely unknown to us, the apostolic faith in Christ had been handed on to the next generation. It remains to be seen what had been gained and lost in the transfer.

[4] Petronius was Nero's 'Arbiter of Taste', and the author of a rather disreputable novel describing low life in southern Italy (only parts now survive). Juvenal was possibly a former civil servant, exiled under Domitian for rude remarks about one of the emperor's favourite slaves. On Domitian's death he returned to Rome, where he lived in poverty and wrote poetry denouncing contemporary society.

2

The new generation

As long as there were men alive who had seen Christ, there was some hope that His teaching might not become corrupted. But inevitably those who had known Him became fewer and fewer. Even while they still lived there were strange practices and ideas abroad (what about baptism for the dead at Corinth?). The crucial test came with the new generation after the last of the men of the apostolic age were dead. The latter years of the first century are almost a total blank, but as we come to the early second century we can see more of the churches by the fitful light shed by various documents. How had they kept the message entrusted to them? What was the next generation like?

There was still a Jewish element in Christianity, but it was fast becoming an errant sect. By the middle of the second century, Justin Martyr could record as a curiosity the existence of Christians who kept all the practices of orthodox Judaism.[1] But he also relates that many regarded them with suspicion. Nor does this suspicion seem to have been groundless. Some of these groups believed that Jesus was merely a man, the greatest of the prophets. They seem to have had a version of Matthew's Gospel, emended to support their own theory, which they circulated in Hebrew. While some of these groups were hardly distinguishable from the erratic Jewish sects, others were definitely Christians. It is from these latter circles, perhaps from Syria, that there comes the first attempt to put church rules into writing.

[1] Justin Martyr, *Dialogue with Trypho* 41. 1-4.

The 'Didache'

Ever since it was brought to light again in the latter part of the nineteenth century, there has been endless debate over the *Didache* (the Teaching of the Twelve Apostles).[2] Whatever its date, by the fourth century it was regarded as sufficiently venerable to be copied and revised, though it was rigorously excluded from the New Testament Canon. The adjective which best describes it is 'quaint'. Dates varying from AD 60 to AD 180 have been suggested for it, but probably somewhere in the early second century is the most likely date.

The work consists of two parts. The first is a series of ethical instructions, framed on a scheme of 'Two Ways' (one leading to life, the other to destruction). Much is based on Jesus' own words, and also on the Old Testament. The second part is concerned with church organization. Baptism is prescribed; the candidates are to be adult (they are told to fast before baptism). The act of baptism is to be in running water, in the threefold name of Father, Son and Holy Spirit. The use of warm water, or even pouring water on the head, is allowed. The Lord's Prayer must be recited three times daily by the Christian. A twice-weekly fast is commanded, but 'not like the hypocrites'. They (the Jews) fast on Monday and Thursday, but the Christians must fast on Wednesday and Friday! Such was the understanding, or rather misunderstanding, of Christ's command.

The public worship of the congregation was centred around a meal, called the 'thanksgiving' or 'eucharist'. Prayers are given, much resembling the Jewish grace at meals, but they are only suggestions. 'Prophets'[3] may give thanks as they feel led. The chief command concerning the Sunday worship is that the worshippers should not have any unresolved grievances.

The most interesting point about the *Didache* is its regulations concerning church officials. Itinerant 'prophets' (?preachers) were expected, and were allowed considerable privileges. The congregation was warned against charlatans

[2] The Greek version was discovered in a manuscript in the Patriarchal Library of Constantinople in 1883. Small fragments on papyrus in both Greek and Coptic have also been found subsequently.
[3] See Glossary, and below, p. 57.

who were only out to make money. Other wandering Christians were to have hospitality, but only for three days; then they were to get a job, or move on. Local officials were to be elected. Their titles ('overseers' and 'servants') have later been ecclesiasticized to 'bishops' and 'deacons'. It speaks volumes for the churches that the two qualities most desired in church leaders were humility, and the lack of a love of money!

The church which drew up the *Didache*, however, did not reckon that its time on earth would be very long. In its prayers it looked forward to the time when God's people will be gathered in; it still used the Aramaic prayer 'Maranatha' (the Aramaic for 'O Lord, come', also used in 1 Corinthians 16:22). Its final chapter is concerned with the signs of the end of the world and Christ's return. Deceivers, false prophets and a fiery trial, conducted by a pseudo-Christ, were confidently expected before the end. As the years went by, many such

The Colosseum, Rome, erected at the end of the 1st century AD, and used for displays of wild beasts and gladiatorial fights. The floor has been excavated to show the cells where the gladiators, prisoners and animals were kept (see detail, right). Ignatius was probably martyred in the Colosseum.

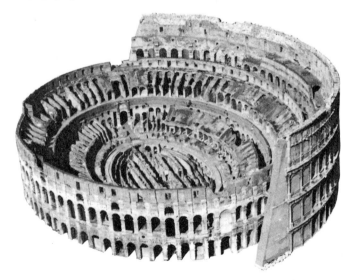

expectations, based on the words of Christ and His apostles, were fulfilled.

Ignatius of Antioch

The first man whose character stands out clearly in the sub-apostolic age is Ignatius of Antioch, in Syria. Our information about him comes from seven of his letters, all written while he was on his way to Rome to be thrown to the wild beasts in the arena (about AD 110). By any reckoning Ignatius was a strange character—although we know of him only from his letters during a hectic journey to Rome as a prisoner, and of course letters dashed off at speed do not necessarily give a fair picture of anyone.

Ignatius was a man with a burning sense of divine commissioning. He lays down the law, and expects it to be obeyed.

Everything is seen by him in terms of black and white. He seems always to be straining forward against any power that would hold him back. But he can generate more heat than light. He whirls off into various extravagant digressions, and then comes back with a domineering attitude which is calculated to discourage the average reader from taking his part. This is the man who had been leader of the church of Antioch, and who was to exercise a brief influence in the churches of Asia Minor.

Apart from his own predicament, Ignatius had two worries: dissension in the churches and the spread of false teaching. And the letters, which were his last will and testament, were to try to settle these problems. Ignatius is usually credited with the invention of the monarchical episcopate (the arrangement of one 'bishop' to rule each congregation), chiefly because he argues for it with every conceivable argument except that it was an apostolic institution. But the monarchical bishop that Ignatius desired is a far cry from the modern diocesan bishop of the Anglican or Roman Catholic pattern. Ignatius's 'bishops' were men chosen from the congregation by election. They remained in one place for life. They were unpaid, and their work was usually limited to looking after one small community. There they would preside at worship each Sunday.

Ignatius was certainly one of the 'prophets', and his words carried considerable weight. Most of the churches that he wrote to had single leaders (the church at Rome being apparently an exception). While he overstated his case concerning the importance of the 'bishop', his motives were simply to preserve order in the various congregations. The alternative to Ignatius's suggestion was the possibility of many small cliques hiving off from the main congregation, or of a running battle for leadership as had already taken place at Corinth.[4] But even such a reasonable suggestion as the appointment of just one leader for each congregation did not pass without challenge. In at least one of the churches Ignatius's prophetic status was questioned when he suggested such an innovation.

Although a forceful personality, Ignatius explicitly denies

[4] See above, pp. 25f.

that he is on the same level as the apostles. He recognizes that Peter and Paul could give orders in a way that he could not, but this does not prevent him giving a strong lead. Perhaps a slight psychological unbalance made him the man that he was. In his letter to the Roman Christians he begs them not to interfere in order to try to spare him from the wild beasts. He has a morbid preoccupation with martyrdom, and uses most bizarre expressions as he tells of his desire to die for Christ. Along with this trait, however, there is also a theological perception of considerable depth.

His theme of unity in the church leads him to stress the 'eucharist' (which he also calls the 'agape' (love-feast) or the 'sacrifice').[5] The fact that the 'eucharist' emphasizes the reality of Christ's body enabled Ignatius to combat the heresy of Docetism, that Jesus' suffering and death were not real, as He only seemed (Greek *dokein*) to be a man. The supporters of this theory seem to have thought that Jesus was some kind of spirit-being, unable to suffer or to be entangled with this real material world. By means of clear assertions of Christ's real incarnation, life and death, supported by appeals to the 'eucharist' which spoke of Christ's body and blood, Ignatius tried to refute the error. By making the 'eucharist', where the 'overseer' or 'bishop' presided, the focus of the church, he also aimed to preserve the unity of the congregations. All in all it was a good rough and ready way of tackling both problems. On sober reflection, it could be seen that it left the way open for certain misconceptions; but few people had the opportunity for sober reflection in those times.

Of the seven genuine letters of Ignatius,[6] six were written to churches. The seventh is written to Polycarp, the 'overseer' of the congregation at Smyrna. Polycarp had a long life, which linked the apostolic age with the great names of the latter part of the second century. As a young man he had listened to the elderly apostle John. When Polycarp himself

[5] Ignatius uses 'eucharist' and 'agape' interchangeably for the communion service; in his time there was no difference, but later the 'agape' became a separate meal.

[6] Six other letters were added later (probably *c.* AD 400). All survive in both Greek and Latin versions. There is also a short recension of three of the genuine letters in Syriac. The genuine letters were disentangled by Archbishop Ussher in 1644, and established as genuine by J. B. Lightfoot in 1882–85.

was a very old man, the church leader Irenaeus was one of his disciples. (We shall hear more of Irenaeus later on.)

Polycarp

Polycarp was still a fairly young man when Ignatius wrote to him, but he was already a capable pastor. He seems to have been a Christian most of his life, and his home church at Smyrna in Asia Minor was a good example of all that a Christian church should be. Polycarp seems to have gained from John, 'the beloved disciple', quite a lot of his gentleness. He stands in marked contrast to Ignatius, as a gentle pastor, although his gentleness was allied to a firm determination which made him inflexible on vital matters. It was to such a man that Ignatius left the task of appointing a new leader for the church at Antioch. When one remembers that the distance from Smyrna to Antioch is somewhere in the region of 500 miles, that communications were sketchy and that there was no public transport, then one can see the magnitude of the task!

Soon after Ignatius's departure under armed guard for Rome, Polycarp was himself in action, writing to the church at Philippi.[7] One of the elders of the congregation at Philippi, Valens by name, had disgraced himself in some financial matters. Valens's wife was involved as well. Polycarp advises the church leaders to mingle judgment with mercy. The pair of wrongdoers were to be sharply disciplined, but were to be received back when they were repentant. To press home the point, Polycarp quotes widely from Paul's letters and invokes Paul's own example. Polycarp, like Ignatius, was conscious that the apostles had an authority greater than his own.

Polycarp also wrote to Philippi to get information; he wanted to have news of the fate of Ignatius and his companions. A further reason for writing was that, like Ignatius, he had to warn the churches against the false teaching which was sweeping that part of the world. Polycarp uses the New Testament more freely than does Ignatius. He quotes from

[7] Polycarp's letter survives only partially in Greek; the deficiencies are supplied from a Latin version. Some scholars think that the letter is really a conflation of two letters, but the reasons are not convincing.

John's letters, and from 1 Peter, as well as from Paul and the Gospels. This was not to be his only brush with heretics. He is later recorded to have called the heretic Marcion[8] 'the first-born of Satan' to his face. On another occasion, finding himself in the public baths at the same time as another heretic, he swiftly called on his friends to depart before the thunderbolt, which the deceiver so richly deserved, destroyed the whole building.

Polycarp was well known throughout the Roman province of Asia as a Christian leader. He led the congregation at Smyrna until an advanced age, and was honoured as far afield as Rome. The local bishop of Rome treated him as a distinguished visitor even though he persisted in celebrating Easter on a different day from the Roman church! But the gracious old man was not allowed to die in peace. At an advanced age (he was at least eighty-six) he was hunted down by the local government officials.[9] They pursued him to a lonely farm in the hills, and he was arrested. A number of other Christians had already been thrown to the wild beasts. The governor of Asia tried to persuade Polycarp to sacrifice to Caesar and so save himself. On being asked to denounce the 'atheists', Polycarp gestured to the screaming mob surrounding the stadium and cried, 'Away with the atheists!' The brave jest was of no avail. He was commanded to curse Christ. The reply he gave will always impress us for its nobility. 'I have served Him for eighty-six years, and He has never done me any wrong', said Polycarp. 'How then can I blaspheme my King who has saved me?' Further pleas and threats were useless. The old man was condemned to be burned alive, and the mob, led by the local Jews, rushed to gather wood for the fire. Polycarp was bound to a stake in the middle of the stadium, and was burnt to death as he prayed. The survivors of the congregation at Smyrna collected his bones, and celebrated 23 February as the anniversary of his martyrdom. A letter was written almost immediately after the martyrdom to the neighbouring congregation in the village of Philomelium, and this is the source of the story.

[8] See Glossary; also below, pp. 52 ff.
[9] The date of Polycarp's martyrdom is uncertain; 155–156, 167 and 177 have all been suggested. On balance 155 or 156 is most likely.

Preaching and teaching in the early second century

From what we can tell, Bible reading and preaching composed much of the programme of the public meetings of the Christian congregations. Three samples of Christian instruction survive from this early period: the homily called *2 Clement*, the *Epistle of Barnabas* and the *Shepherd*, written by the Roman visionary Hermas. Each has its own interesting slant, though none of them can be called great literature.

The writer of *2 Clement* was a practical man. He reminds his audience in general terms of what God has done for them, and then devotes most of his space to explaining what sort of conduct is suitable for Christians. He reminds them of the coming judgment, as an additional reason for avoiding sin; and he delivers a sharp rebuke to people who profess to be Christians but live no differently from their pagan neighbours.

Whoever wrote the *Epistle of Barnabas* was of a more speculative frame of mind. He has at least some connection with the circles where the *Didache* was used, since he concludes his work with a summary based on the scheme of the Two Ways (this also forms the first part of the *Didache*, as we have seen). The main theme of 'Barnabas' is a spiritualization of the Mosaic law. The writer holds that the Jews were wrong to take the Old Testament literally. It all had a spiritual meaning which pointed to Jesus, and that was its sole purpose. So he proceeds to allegorize everything in the Old Testament to give it a Christian meaning. Some attempts are vaguely plausible, as when 'Barnabas' says that the blessing of Manasses and Ephraim (where the younger receives a greater blessing than the elder) prefigures God's attitude to the Jews and Gentiles. But the majority of examples are totally improbable, such as his explanation that the food-laws of Leviticus and Deuteronomy really mean the prohibition of various vices!

The *Shepherd of Hermas* is the oddest of these three works, and it will probably remain a mystery why it almost rivalled parts of the New Testament for popularity. It was so popular that the Muratorian Canon (a list of acknowledged books of the

Countryside in Asia Minor (modern Turkey). Polycarp's farm would have been in country of this sort.

New Testament from the second half of the second century)[1] needed to exclude it from the list of books to be read in church, on the grounds that it was not apostolic (just as we enjoy *Pilgrim's Progress* but do not put it on the same level as Scripture).

Hermas, the author of the *Shepherd*, seems to have had a varied career. Starting life as a slave, he acquired his freedom, and became quite wealthy, but subsequently he lost his wealth and endured some sort of persecution. But he was well connected among the Christians at Rome, for his brother, Pius, became the leader ('bishop') of the congregation there.

Hermas's book is cast in the form of a series of parables and visions, but its underlying purpose (as with *2 Clement* and the *Epistle of Barnabas*) is to tackle a problem of practical Christian living. With Hermas the problem is purity of Christian life. While all Christians would agree that at baptism all past sins were blotted out, what was to happen to those within the ranks of the churches who committed really grave sins after baptism? Were these able to be forgiven? Hermas claims that he has had a revelation from God, to the effect that there is one further chance offered. Persistent sin after baptism is ruled out as inadmissible; but forgiveness is possible for serious offences once, and once only, after public confession and penance. Strange to say, Hermas received most criticism for being too lax!

The early advances of Christianity

So far we have seen what was happening in Asia Minor and Rome, with a sidelong glance at Syria, from where Ignatius came. What of Christians elsewhere?

There were certainly some in Egypt. Not only is there the case of Apollos from the New Testament,[2] but the first fragment of a New Testament book comes from Egypt. This is the famous Rylands fragment of John's Gospel, datable by the evidence of handwriting to the first decades of the second

---

[1] See Glossary. The whole of the fragment is translated in J. Stevenson (editor), *A New Eusebius* (SPCK, 1957), pp. 144–147.
[2] See Acts 18:24.

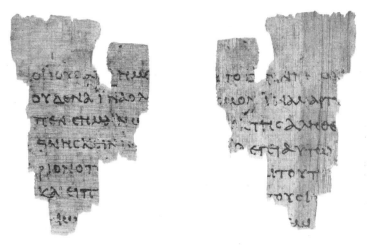

Papyrus fragment of the Fourth Gospel in Greek (the 'Rylands Fragment'), found in Egypt. Dating from the first half of the 2nd century AD, it is the earliest known fragment of the New Testament in any language. The photograph shows both sides of the fragment. John Rylands Library, Manchester.

century.[3] Various other fragments of papyrus, containing either bits of canonical Gospels or very early composite accounts of Jesus' life, come from second-century Egypt.[4] By no means all Egyptian Christians were of the main stream of the faith, however; some early heretics also came from Egypt (see chapter 3). But until the last years of the second century we have no definite details about Christians in Egypt.

Of Christianity in mainland Greece we have no other information beyond the goings-on at Corinth and the little light shed on Philippi by Polycarp's letter. One other area which may have first received Christians at this time is southern France. Certainly there were well-established Christian congregations at Lyons and Vienne in AD 177 when they were the victims of a particularly vicious outbreak of persecution.[5] One of the church leaders martyred at that time was then aged

[3] It is now the chief exhibit of the John Rylands Library, Manchester.
[4] See H. I. Bell and T. C. Steat (editors), *Fragments of an Unknown Gospel and Other Early Christian Papyri* (British Museum, 1935); also C. H. Roberts in *Journal of Theological Studies*, new series, vol. xvi, pp. 183–185.
[5] Eusebius, *Church History* v. 1. 3–63.

Map 2

The Eastern Area

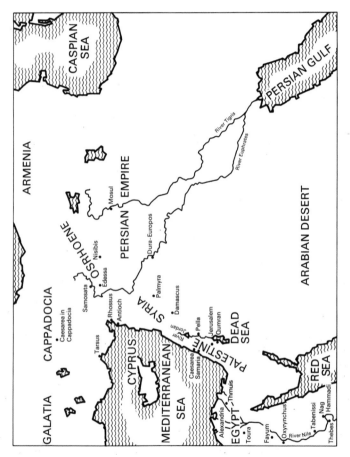

ninety. He may well have come to southern France as a young man. The earliest French Christians almost certainly came from Asia Minor; and the links with the home congregations were kept up.

The Syriac-speaking Christians

What about the lands east of Syria? Beyond the Roman frontiers were the kingdoms of Edessa and Armenia, and the Parthian Empire. Speaking a language very close to the vernacular that Christ Himself used,[6] this area would seem wide open to the Christian gospel. Unfortunately, our information comes mainly from much later writers. Stories like that of King Abgar of Edessa, who is supposed to have written to Jesus, must be dismissed as pleasant romances. We know that native Syriac Christianity was distinctly odd to the eyes of Greek Christians. They muttered about the taint of the Gnostic heresy,[7] and viewed its extreme rigorism with suspicion and distaste. By the end of the second century, there were certainly two factions in that part of the world. The younger and more orthodox (to Greek eyes) was initiated from Antioch, and led by Palut of Edessa (he was made 'bishop' *c.* AD 190).[8] The older, and probably indigenous, faction was associated with the name of Tatian (Adai in Syriac),[9] but it probably went back well before his career in the second half of the second century.

Attempts have been made to find links between the community of the Dead Sea Scrolls and the Syriac-speaking churches. But it is more likely that such similarities as there are between the two groups are the product of a common background and outlook. The rigorous spirit of James the Lord's brother and the Jerusalem church of before AD 70 seems to have been inherited by the Christians of East Syria and beyond the frontier of the Roman Empire.

[6] Syriac is the eastern dialect of Aramaic. Palestinian Aramaic, which Jesus used, was the western dialect.

[7] See Glossary, and below, pp. 47 ff.

[8] Information from *Doctrina Addai*, a work of uncertain date from Edessa. The relevant part is translated in J. Stevenson, *A New Eusebius*, pp. 152–153.

[9] See further pp. 56, 84.

Their subsequent career is a fascinating forgotten episode of Christian history.[1] Branded as heretics in the fifth century for supporting the outspoken and unlucky patriarch of Constantinople, Nestorius, they retreated beyond the reach of Byzantine persecutors.[2] Their main centres of learning were first at Edessa and then at Nisibis, further east. Their missionaries went south to India, and had spread across mainland Asia to China by the sixth century. The rise of Islam effectively cut them off from other Christians, for whom they survived as the myth of Prester John, the Christian priest-king of the far east who would one day come to crush the hordes of Islam. They had contributed monasticism to Tibet, and left monuments in China before their network of churches collapsed

[1] There is no standard work on Syriac Christianity in English. Short notices occur in S. C. Neill, *Christian Missions* (Penguin Books, 1964), pp. 48–55, 94–97. W. Wright, *History of Syriac Literature* (1898) is old but still useful.
[2] Nestorius was condemned in AD 431 for teaching that there were two entirely separate natures in Christ.

John's Gospel in Syriac, a language close to the Aramaic spoken by Jesus. This manuscript dates from the 5th century AD, and contains John 6:53–64. British Museum, London.

under the hammering of Ghengiz Khan and Tamberlane in the twelfth to fourteenth centuries. One branch survived as the Mar Thoma church of South India (still using a Syriac liturgy which was as incomprehensible to the natives as was Latin to the mediaeval peasants). Other scattered congregations remained in the hills around Mosul, in North Iraq, enduring continual harassment and persecution from the Turks, until recent times, when they were rediscovered as a romantic survival in the last years of the nineteenth century. Oriental Christianity forms one of the great might-have-beens of history.

Pliny and the Christians

Asia Minor provides us with one more glimpse of the early churches, this time through the eyes of an enemy. The younger Pliny was really a wealthy Roman man of letters; if he had been alive in Victorian times, he would have been the typical squire who dabbled in science and the arts. However, by virtue of his rank as a senator, much against his will he was sent to govern Bithynia in about AD 112. He was the typical irresolute bureaucrat (someone has called him 'the archetypal red-tapeworm'), consulting the emperor on every trivial matter possible (local fire brigades, for example). The Christians were one of his many administrative headaches.[3]

Pliny found that his execution of confessed Christians had led to all sorts of people being accused. Certainly Christians were widespread, and Pliny laments the deserted temples and infrequency of sacrifices. He interviewed a considerable number of former Christians, and was puzzled by what he learned. He obtained information of meetings before daybreak when Christ was worshipped as a god. There was also secret oath-taking, but the oath (*sacramentum*) which they took was to abstain from harming others! Their meals, he reports, were entirely innocent; and in this he was probably refuting rumours of cannibalism and incest. The only church officials whom he could find or catch were two 'deaconesses'; he tortured them to discover the truth, but all he could find

[3]Pliny, *Epistles* x. 96, 97. Translation in J. Stevenson, *A New Eusebius*, pp. 13–16.

was what he called 'extravagant superstition'. However, Pliny was worried. All sorts of people were involved, including numbers of Roman citizens. So he wrote to the emperor Trajan for advice.

The imperial reply survives, and was later circulated sufficiently for it to come into the hands of a Christian lawyer from North Africa, who scathingly denounces it for inconsistency. The emperor dissuades Pliny from conducting witch-hunts, but states clearly that Christians brought before the courts must recant or be punished. Such remained the official line for over a century—and there were more than a few emperors who would appease unruly provincials by conducting a witch-hunt for Christians to provide entertainment in the arena.

Marble bust of the emperor Trajan, who wrote to Pliny about the Christians *c.* 112. British Museum, London.

3

The way-out men

Many people think that the study of ancient heresies has no relevance today. There is some truth in this, because the ancient heresies of the second century are quite dead, and will not revive in their former shapes. Others, who have read a little church history, see modern errors as reincarnations of ancient heresies. While this is not completely true, it at least means that ancient battles over the Christian faith are re-examined with a view to making use of any help that they can give. No ancient heresy is reproduced in every detail in our modern age, but certain basic types recur with almost monotonous regularity, if only because there are a limited number of basic ways of tampering with received truth.

It has been said that the church's greatest theologians were heretics. By this it is meant that the most lively brains were most likely to attempt to 'improve' the traditional statements of belief, and in so doing many went wildly off course. The temptation to try was obvious, especially if a man had a smattering of contemporary philosophy, or an inclination towards the mysterious and occult, with mystic revelations and secret writings. The first group we will meet are a very varied crowd, and modern church historians have classified them all under the general name of 'Gnostic'.[1] This is an umbrella-term to include all those of this period who professed to have some secret revelation or knowledge, and it contains within its range both those on the borders of mainstream Christianity and those whose doctrine was mainly pagan mysticism garnished with a few Christian ideas and phrases. The ancient writers were more ready to recognize the differ-

[1] See Glossary.

ences between various Gnostic teachers, and many of those whom we lump together as Gnostics fought each other. It is often hard to see where erratic Christianity ended and heresy began, but we will use the term 'Gnostic' to cover all schemes where salvation depended on having some secret knowledge.

The similarities between these heresies and some modern cults may be noted. Some Gnostic sects had secret writings in addition to the Bible (*cf.* Mormonism). Others had special, and very strange, interpretations of the actual Scriptures (*cf.* Jehovah's Witnesses) based on a non-biblical system. Others used Christianity as merely one of several revelations (*cf.* Theosophy). Most were of the type of error which adds to the basic revelation, so as to distort it; but in Marcion we have an early example of a reductionist, who cut down the Christian revelation to suit his own theory (*cf.* both pre-Barthian and post-Barthian liberalism). The common factor with all of them was the imposing of a foreign system on the biblical data.

We have already seen the earliest signs of the warping of Christianity under pressure from a variety of outside forces. One has only to read Juvenal's *Satires*[2] to realize that there were many religions for sale in imperial Rome, and that the Roman man-in-the-street tended to be mildly interested or loftily contemptuous of all of them. The further east you went, the greater the tendency to have a bit of each, and to agree that all were really going to the same destination. Artemis of the Ephesians, the Phrygian Magna Mater, Egyptian Isis, the Bona Dea of Rome and the nameless fertility goddesses of the West could all get along together in cosmopolitan tolerance. People could be initiated into various secret cults without feeling that such divided allegiance was incongruous. Each made their contribution, and (according to Juvenal) expected their fee. Could not Jesus take his place with Mithras, Orpheus, Yahweh and others?

Or perhaps the real secret of Christianity was allowed only to those initiated into the secret teachings which Christ was supposed to have left to certain trusted intimates. This secret gospel gave the true inner meaning to the publicly-read Scriptures. Or perhaps one rose beyond the world of the God

[2] Especially *Satire* vi. 511–592.

Column from the Temple of Artemis, Ephesus. This massive temple, one of the 'seven wonders' of the ancient world, may originally have been dedicated to an Eastern goddess whom the Greeks adopted under the name of Artemis. British Museum, London.

of the Old Testament, into a purer and more refined world where God did not dirty His hands with the material universe, but was lofty and apart, perceived only dimly by the enlightened. Yet again, there might be direct revelations given later than apostolic times, with God speaking again to newer prophets who were about to usher in the New Jerusalem. Gnosticism could include any or all of these ingredients in any permutation.

Most heresies were attempts to alter the traditional Christian faith to make it more acceptable to contemporary

49

thought. Mainstream Christians noted that, apart from Marcionites, few of the sects produced martyrs. Some even encouraged denial and apostasy in the face of persecution.

It is impossible to tell when the first aberration from apostolic doctrine began. Certainly, it was soon after the first congregation gathered at Jerusalem. Many of the ancients ascribed all heresy to Simon Magus.[3] There had been an undercurrent in Judaism of speculation and philosophical manipulation of the faith. To the Jew, as long as you did what was right, there was plenty of elbow-room for theological speculation. There was also a love of the mysterious, common to all human beings, and an interest in secret doctrines and rites. All this produced a congenial climate for remoulding the New Testament faith so that it would be in closer accord with any given feeling and ideas. Paul and John had denounced the first signs of it. Polycarp and Ignatius had declared war on it. The next generation holds the big names who aimed to bring the Christian churches behind them in their modification of truth.

The Roman historian Tacitus and the satirist Juvenal had both complained that all forms of Eastern depravity collected in Rome. The Christian congregations there could well have uttered a similar complaint, for the two most outstanding heretics of the early second century both came to Rome to propagate their ideas, although both were born elsewhere.

Valentinus

Valentinus came from Alexandria, but settled in Rome at the same time that Hermas[4] was writing. He was soon noted for his learning, and apparently very nearly became bishop![5] It was only after this hope had been disappointed that he formed his own sect. At this time the Christian community in Rome must have been composed of various small cells with little contact between each other. Justin Martyr tells us that he held classes for instruction in an upstairs room of a private

[3] See Acts 8:9 ff.
[4] See above, pp. 39 f.
[5] Tertullian, *Against the Valentinians* iv; Irenaeus, *Against Heresies* iii. 4. 3.

house.[6] Later on, Polycarp could visit an expatriate Asian community who even celebrated Easter on a different date from the rest of the Roman Christians.[7] A learned and eloquent man could soon gather a group of disciples.

From the discoveries of manuscripts at Nag Hammadi in Egypt[8] we can get an idea of Valentinus's own teaching; the *Gospel of Truth* in the Jung Codex is almost certainly his work. Irenaeus gives us a later version of Valentinus's system. The *Gospel of Truth* preaches a Christianity in the form of esoteric, or secret, knowledge. The root of the trouble with the human race is ignorance, not sin. Jesus is thought of in terms of a

[6] *Acta of Justin* 3, cited by J. Stevenson, *A New Eusebius*, p. 29.
[7] Eusebius, *Church History* iv. 17. 7; v. 24. 8.
[8] The full story of the find is told in F. L. Cross (editor), *The Jung Codex* (Mowbray, 1955). The find was made in about 1945, but the MSS were lost except one which went to the Jung Institute in Zürich. The remainder are now in Cairo, and are gradually being published.

A manuscript of the Gnostic Valentinus's teaching, in a Coptic dialect. Late 4th or early 5th century, from the British Museum, London.

revealer of secret knowledge of God. Salvation is thought of in terms of having this secret knowledge. It is like Hermas, but without the strong moral tone, and without the clear images. The overwhelming impression of this, and of most other Gnostic works, is of vagueness, word-spinning and tedium. In their system Christianity becomes a vague sort of theosophy.

Valentinus later developed his system, according to Irenaeus, into a complex hierarchy of spirit-beings, setting a trail from an unknown incomprehensible God through a series of thirty spiritual beings to a fallen Wisdom who was responsible for producing the god that created the material world. Salvation consisted in escaping from enslavement to this world, although the majority of men were inextricably enmeshed in it, and most Christians (except Valentinus's coterie) would never completely escape. The language of the New Testament survives, but the words used are merely connotation-words, invested with a totally different meaning. New Testament allusions abound in the *Gospel of Truth*, but never an actual quotation. At its worst, the whole system seems to be a game of numerology, using the New Testament as the quarry for the numbers.

Under various disciples, whom we shall meet later, the system of Valentinus was elaborated. Their tedious and obscure writings survive in the refutations composed by their enemies, and in occasional finds in the Egyptian sands. Such fantasies will always have their devotees, but (as Irenaeus said) to describe them is to refute them.

Marcion

Marcion posed a more serious problem to the early Christians because he was much closer to them. He did not bother with the cosmological speculations which fascinated Valentinus and company, although his debt to such people should not be overlooked. He was a second-generation Christian, born the son of a church leader in Sinope, in north-east Asia Minor on the Black Sea Coast.[9] He made a considerable fortune in the shipping trade, and when he came to Rome it was perhaps his

[9] Our main source of information about Marcion is Tertullian's attack on him, *Against Marcion.*

money that dazzled. Dubious company (theologically) led him to formulate a system which caused him to be put out of fellowship, and he formed his own organization. His following was to last into the mediaeval period, though he himself is said to have thought better of his theories in later life. However, church discipline was strict; he was told that he must bring back all those whom he had led astray. He died unreconciled.

Marcion was ardently anti-Judaistic and pro-Paul. From his Gnostic friends he had learned to distinguish sharply between the God of the Old Testament and the unknown God who was the Father of Jesus Christ. He reckoned the God of the Old Testament to be considerably inferior to Jesus, though he did not go as far as to reckon Him evil. Any tendencies towards Judaism, or any Old Testament borrowings, were anathema to him. Consequently, he made great use of Paul, especially in his anti-Judaistic and anti-legalistic passages.

Naturally, Marcion found much in the New Testament which did not fit his theories; and that was so much the worse for the New Testament. Although there was no formal list of canonical books at this time (c. AD 140), most of what we now know as the New Testament was acknowledged as authoritative. People could quote Christ's words from the Gospels, or the injunctions of His apostles (e.g. Paul, Peter, John), and know that these would settle an argument.[1] Marcion started the trend which has had many followers right up to the present —if it doesn't suit the theory, excise it as spurious or an interpolation.

When Marcion went to work on the New Testament, only Luke's Gospel survived from the canonical four; and even this needed considerable alteration before it suited Marcion. He cut out all the narratives of Jesus' birth, and other references to His humanity and Jewishness. The only apostle allowed was Paul, and then only after Marcion had thrown out the Pastoral Epistles and excised certain other awkward passages. By a strange freak, some of Marcion's prologues to Paul's letters have survived in some Latin manuscripts of the

[1] *1 Clement* and Polycarp are good early examples.

Vulgate.[2] With a lawyer's thoroughness, Tertullian goes through Marcion's 'New Testament' pointing out all the changes with almost ghoulish delight. But in spite of such a hammering, Marcionism appealed to those of a rationalistic frame of mind, and it remained as a nasty irritant to mainstream Christianity.

The later followers of Valentinus

Once it had been formulated, Marcion's system did not admit of many modifications. But Valentinus was followed by many who improved on his system. Ptolemy probably worked up the spiritual hierarchy which Valentinus had invented. One small work of his survives, a letter to a lady called Flora.[3] It is a surprisingly sane work, dealing with the different values of various parts of the Mosaic law. He distinguishes between the moral law (which has permanent validity), the law of retaliation (superceded by Christ's law of love) and the ceremonial law (spiritualized by Jesus). He then deduces that the Mosaic law was the work of the inferior creator, and not of the supreme God!

Valentinus had used John's Gospel as a quarry for his speculations, giving special attention to the prologue of that Gospel. This interest in the Fourth Gospel was continued by Heracleon, who wrote an early commentary on it.[4] Only fragments of his work survive, quoted in other works by those who wanted to refute his system. A list of quotations is all that survives from another author, Theodotus, who may have been the leader of a sect which tried to harmonize Christianity and Aristotelianism.[5]

Syria produced its own brand of Gnostic heresy. The leader here was Basilides. He had something in common with Valentinus in that he thought of the supreme God as unknow-

[2] See F. L. Cross, *The Early Christian Fathers* (Duckworth, 1960), pp. 64–65.
[3] Translated in full in J. Stevenson, *A New Eusebius*, pp. 91–95.
[4] Because Gnostics were so interested in John's Gospel, certain Christians at Rome, led by an elder called Gaius, suspected that it had been written by a heretic and tried to have it banned!
[5] The scientific philosophy of Aristotle, the tutor of Alexander the Great in the fourth century BC.

able, but he separated Him from the God of the Jews by 365 heavens, each emanating from the previous one. A strong strain of Docetism[6] appears in his ideas, for he believed that Jesus was not crucified. He said that Simon of Cyrene was mistaken for Jesus and crucified in His stead. His whole system was much less Christian than that of Valentinus. Valentinus held that Jesus was still some sort of 'Saviour', but Basilides thought that confession of Christ crucified could be bettered by secret knowledge of the plan of the 'unknown Father'.[7]

Valentinus and Basilides may have seemed to be on the extreme fringe, but there were others even further out! The early chapters of Genesis provided fruitful ground for speculation. Some people, called the Ophites or Naasenes, worshipped the serpent in the garden of Eden story, believing it to be the emissary from the unknown God sent to liberate mankind from the power of the evil creator of the material world.

One sect[8] even made Pharaoh, Ahab and Jezebel saints, with Moses, Elijah and the prophets as sinners! Others,[9] reckoning the material world to be worthless, counted it right to despise it and practise all sorts of immorality. Some other sects[1] had secret revelations from alleged angelic beings, and their content was hardly Christian even in name. Some, such as Marcus, who practised his arts in Asia Minor and perhaps in southern France, were little more than magicians and conjurors. Certain Gnostics are said to have had painted images and to have worshipped them in the same way as did pagans. Others taught strange rituals[2] and passwords, by which the initiate could pass through the various heavenly spheres to paradise. The fringe of extravagant cults which clung about the churches could contain almost any weird system of beliefs.[3]

[6] See above, p. 35.
[7] The above account of Basilides comes from Irenaeus. Hippolytus gives a widely differing version, with three emanations from the 'unknown Father', the lowest of which creates the god who made the world.
[8] Cainites; also attributed to Marcion by Irenaeus.
[9] Carpocratians, Nicolaitans.
[1] Elchesites, so called from Elchesai, their heavenly emissary.
[2] The Ophite diagrams described by Celsus and Origen.
[3] The best modern survey of Gnosticism, giving a great many texts translated into English, is R. M. Grant (editor), Gnosticism : an Anthology (Collins, 1961).

Classified in among these people, but differing from them, were the Syriac-speaking teachers such as Tatian and Bard-aisan. Tatian (the Greek form of the Syriac Adai) was a disciple of Justin Martyr, the converted philosopher who flourished at Rome in the mid-second century. (We shall hear more of Justin when we look at those who wrote in the defence of Christianity.)[4] Tatian has left one work in Greek, a vitriolic attack on contemporary paganism, but he appears to have written in Syriac as well. He is most famous for his *Diatessaron* (Greek for 'by four'), the four Gospels combined into a single narrative by a scissors-and-paste method. The version was very popular in the East Syrian churches. Apart from a tiny fragment in Greek, which was discovered in the ruins of Dura-Europos on the Euphrates, nothing has survived of the work. But commentaries were written on it (one, by Ephrem Syrus of the late fourth century, survives), and it was only in the mid-fifth century that it was suppressed because of supposed heretical tendencies. The separated Gospels in Syriac did not gain prominence until after this, when the Old Syriac versions were revised into the Peshitta version in the late fifth century.[5]

Tatian revolted against the paganism of his parents, and encouraged a rigorous asceticism. He condemned marriage,[6] and is apparently the first to have forbidden the use of wine at the 'eucharist', substituting water. Tatian is said by his enemies to have held that Adam was eternally damned, this being their most serious accusation against him. His followers, called Encratites (the Controlled Ones), spread rapidly in East Syria. Perhaps one of his converts was Bardaisan, who was born in Edessa and was converted in about 179. Bardaisan was strongly against the determinism of much Greek philosophy, and he strongly attacked Marcion. He is also the first known Syriac hymn-writer. Like Tatian, he was an enthusiastic missionary, and the Syriac-speaking churches probably owed much of their strength to leaders like these. Despite the fact that they came under the suspicion of Greek Christian

---

[4] See below, pp. 81 ff.

[5] For Syriac versions of the New Testament, see B. M. Metzger, *The Text of the New Testament* (Oxford University Press, 1964), pp. 68–71.

[6] In some East Syrian churches it is believed that celibacy was a condition of church membership!

writers, these men were probably mainly orthodox Christians with a number of odd ideas.

Montanus

The order of 'prophets' had been an outstanding feature of the churches from the earliest days. These people were men or women with special abilities of spiritual insight and teaching. Philip the evangelist had four daughters who were all so gifted.[7] Ignatius was a later example of a Christian 'prophet', and there were occasional 'prophets' in Syria and Asia Minor until well into the second century. Naturally, the local congregations could not rely on the ministrations of these itinerant preachers, and so made arrangements to run their churches with elected officials. This may have resulted in friction between the travelling 'prophet' and the church elders, but a visit from a 'prophet' could be very welcome. As early as the *Didache*, however, the abuses were obvious.[8] The latter part of the second century saw the rise of a movement which effectively discredited all 'prophets'.

It is not without significance that the movement called Montanism began in Phrygia, where ecstatic worship had long been associated with pagan deities.[9] In a remote congregation in Phrygia a man called Montanus went into a frenzy. The people there thought it was a case of demon-possession, and even tried to cast out the devil. Montanus claimed that it was the Holy Spirit speaking through him. He was joined by two women, Priscilla and Maximilla, who also underwent similar experiences, and offered various pronouncements as the living voice of the Holy Spirit speaking to the churches. Tied to this ecstatic utterance was a strong expectation of the last days, and the 'prophets' even suggested that the New Jerusalem would be set up in two obscure Phrygian villages.

But enthusiasm cut no ice with the staid leaders of the congregations. They were not impressed by the antics of Montanus and his friends. In circles where purity of life was often

[7] Acts 21 :8, 9.
[8] See above, pp. 31 f.
[9] Eusebius, *Church History* v. 14–19 is the main account of Montanism. It includes many extracts from writers who knew the movement at first hand.

the greatest test of truth, Montanus and his followers were not shining examples. Both Priscilla and Maximilla had deserted their husbands; other leaders were noted for their greed; one was condemned by the local Roman governor as a common thief. The Montanists had a poor record of steadfastness under persecution; and their prophecies were incoherent ravings.[1] Their habit of paying their officials (for Montanism soon set up its own organization) was especially frowned upon.

In its mad Phrygian form Montanism soon largely burned itself out. The original 'prophets' died, and the end of the world did not come. But a more sober and ethically strict form survived in places, and later Tertullian was to join them. But over against the wild doings of the later Roman Empire, the Christians were becoming almost a Puritanical sect. The great virtues for them were those of decency and law and order, and the Christian life was expected to be sober and staid. To the thoughtful pagan, disgusted by the flagrant immorality and dishonesty then current, such a form of Christianity was very attractive. What was lost was the exuberance of the early days. But it is questionable whether a frenziedly emotional faith could have withstood the attacks of imperial Rome, or have eventually even claimed an emperor as a supporter.

The effect of the wild aberrations of the second century was small in comparison to the space often devoted to them by later scholars. The improbable systems, based on secret revelations, had an appeal to the sort of person who today would be an ardent cultist. Some members were lost to the mainstream churches,[2] but the sects never had much chance of taking over mainstream Christianity. The movement was largely ephemeral, although little congregations of Valentinians and others occur as late as the fifth century.

But the rise of the Gnostics did give the stimulus for two useful things. First of all, with Gnostic teachers hawking their various systems, Christians from the mainstream churches had to take a long hard look at their beliefs. Even if, as Irenaeus said, you only had to describe the Gnostic systems to refute them, the task needed doing. Aspiring Christian

[1] Examples in J. Stevenson, *A New Eusebius*, p. 113.
[2] *E.g.* Florinus, to whom Irenaeus wrote a letter, preserved by Eusebius.

writers set to work, both to demolish the theology of the Gnostics and also to work out mainstream theology in more detail.[3] This was a great help for the churches.

Secondly, there was a movement to give explicit recognition to the books of the New Testament.[4] This came about through reaction to the use made of 'secret writings'. The writings of Valentinus, Basilides and their successors, though tedious at best and at worst unreadable, had achieved some circulation. There were spurious gospels, prophecies and revelations (but strangely few forged epistles). These needed exclusion, or the churches would find people getting up and reading the *Gospel of Truth* or the *Secret Book of John*. It was not that the apocryphal Scriptures rivalled the New Testament; as one scholar[5] rightly said, they did not need excluding because they excluded themselves. They are all far inferior to the New Testament in both style and content. But it was necessary to put down in black and white what was actually accepted as Scripture.

As the danger of the sects passed, certain churches seem to have taken over their love of speculation. In Alexandria, it may have been that orthodox Christians decided that the answer to bad speculation was Bible-based speculation. Certainly this approach seems to have drawn back many supporters of the sects (*e.g.* Origen's patron Ambrose).[6] Elsewhere, determined refutation and deeper instruction of church members halted the inroads of the cults. So, in spite of uncertain communications which would have left many congregations with only their own abilities to face Gnostics, the scattered congregations survived their first ideological battle pretty well. It speaks volumes for the vitality of their faith that they could do so.

---

[3] See further below, pp. 60 ff.
[4] See further below, pp. 63 ff.
[5] M. R. James, *The Apocryphal New Testament* (Oxford University Press, 1953), pp. xi-xii. This is the best collection of extra-canonical writings in English.
[6] See Glossary; also below, p. 123.

Within the body of Christ

Irenaeus

Irenaeus has come into our story so many times already, that it is probably time to tell his own story. He came from the seaport of Smyrna, to whose church the apostle John sent the letter recorded in Revelation 2. He was a member of the congregation where Polycarp presided, and as a young man he had actually heard the elderly Polycarp describe how he had heard the apostle John preach. Irenaeus describes the old days nostalgically in a letter written to a friend, Florinus, who had once been a keen Christian but had subsequently become involved with a Gnostic sect. Irenaeus may have had friends among the Christians in southern France. Certainly he was well known to them, and after a vicious persecution in Lyons[1] he went there to become the 'overseer' of that Christian congregation. This was in AD 177, when he must have been well into middle life. He was well experienced in mediation in difficult situations. He had interceded for some Montanists while still in Asia Minor, and he later gave a sharp rebuke to Victor, bishop of Rome, for his high-handed attempt to excommunicate the Christians of Asia Minor. He worked hard in France, apparently even learning some of the vernacular Celtic. His main claim to fame, however, is his ponderous work in refutation of Gnosticism (*Against the Heresies*). The actual refutation covers only the first two books of the five into which the work is divided; the remainder covers various points of Christian theology. It gives the impression of having been written piecemeal; this may be so, as Irenaeus seems to have had a very active life. His work on heresies was justly popular.

[1] See below, pp. 87 ff.

Within a generation it had been circulated in Egypt (papyrus fragments of a copy have been found which date from the early third century). It was also soon translated into Latin; this version is one of the earliest Christian documents in Latin.

Irenaeus's aim was practical. He wanted to unmask the theosophy of Gnosticism for the rubbish that it was. And he wanted to show what Christianity was really about, and from what source you could get a good account of it. He was in a position to pass on interesting information as to the sources of the four Gospels. To him it was axiomatic that there should be four, and only four, Gospels. It was as obvious as having four points of the compass. The guarantee that apostolic truth had been handed down without alteration, as against the Gnostic claims of secret traditions, is provided by the continuous teaching of the major churches. Irenaeus could look back to his teacher Polycarp, and behind him to the apostle John. Other churches, such as the church at Rome which he cites as an example, could point to a line of teachers reaching back to the apostles. Each in turn had proclaimed the apostolic doctrine. The facts were public knowledge, and clear for all to see. The succession that Irenaeus wanted to establish was a succession of preachers. It was not even essential for his argument that each should have been taught by the previous one, let alone that each had been ordained by the previous one (ordination is never mentioned). His argument was that the apostolic gospel was what had been preached in all the main churches from the time of the apostles until now. It was a good argument for him to use while he was within 150 years of the resurrection. It was not a good argument for much beyond this, when any venerable tradition might be hopefully ascribed to the apostles.

Irenaeus's theology

What did Christianity mean to Irenaeus? First, it was a definite body of truth, handed down from Christ and the apostles. This body of truth, which some early writers call the 'rule of faith', contained statements about God, about His intervention through Jesus Christ, the main facts of Jesus' life, death and resurrection, and the purpose of His coming.

It would also explain Christ's call to repent and believe, and detail the results of accepting or rejecting Him. Although Irenaeus was not anti-intellectual, he set greater store by acceptance of God's revelation than by ability to have slick intellectual answers for everything. There is a streak of authoritarianism in Irenaeus, in his appeal to the body of truth as taught by the principal congregations of Christians.

Irenaeus put especial emphasis on the reality of Jesus' incarnation. In this he was following in the footsteps of Ignatius and Polycarp in combatting the prevalent heresy of Docetism from Asia Minor. This heresy, as we have seen, effectively made Jesus a disembodied spirit, and wrote off the entire physical world as evil.[2] The reaction to this gives Irenaeus the particular slant of his theology, namely that Christ with a real human body was the first of a new creation into which believers were born again. The heretics had denied that Jesus had a real human body. Irenaeus retorted that unless Jesus did have a real human body, salvation would be impossible. Looking for common ground from which to denounce the idea of a phantasmal Christ, Irenaeus fastens on the teaching of the communion or eucharist, where the reality of Christ's body is clearly stated.

Irenaeus's idea of salvation had its roots in the Pauline idea of Christ as the second Adam. To Irenaeus, Jesus is the first of a new humanity. God has been fully united with the flesh of man in Jesus, and therefore those who come to Christ are incorporated into a new race. He even works out the comparison of Christ and Adam down to the details. Christ corresponds to Adam, Mary to Eve, the cross to the tree in the garden of Eden. The sufferings of Jesus are viewed in the light of the total obedience needed to inaugurate a new and perfect human race. The final division of the two races is to take place at the last judgment, but until then there is every chance of changing sides.

Such a theology has obvious strengths and weaknesses. It leaves the sufferings and death of Christ as of secondary importance to His incarnation, and it opens the way to a sacramentalism whereby people could be formally incorpor-

[2] This rejection of the material world as evil, and the belief in a purely spirit-being as Christ, was also found in many Gnostic sects.

ated into the congregation without much in the way of a personal faith. Its strong points are the insistence on Jesus as a real human being at one with us, the emphasis on the act of God in making salvation possible, and the over-all stress on Christianity as a system of truth. This theology, like many others, was shaped in part as a result of the surrounding pressures which acted upon the theologian. This particular emphasis appealed to Irenaeus, and it constantly occurs in both his surviving works (*Against the Heresies* and the *Demonstration of the Apostolic Teaching*).

The Canon of the New Testament

Irenaeus, in the course of his works, had emphatically stated that there could only be four Gospels, so ruling out the 'Fifth Gospel', the *Gospel of Truth* of Valentinus. As we have seen, the challenge of Gnosticism hastened the production of a definite list of those books which were acknowledged as forming the New Testament. The term 'New Testament' was not yet used, but there was a gradual demarcation of the books which were to be read in public worship. Even before the last days of the first century, Papias had put a very high value on authentic pronouncements from the apostles. In *1 Clement*[3] the words of Jesus and the commands of Paul are quoted with just as much authority as the Old Testament. The term 'the Scriptures' was normally kept for the Old Testament, but it was gradually extended to cover the New Testament as well.

In ancient times books were written on scrolls, and the Old Testament was no exception to this practice. But a newer form of book was coming into use just as the New Testament writings were beginning to be copied. This was the notebook or 'codex' form, which is the format used for all modern books. From the very start this form was used for the New Testament writings,[4] and gradually Old Testament books were also written on the codex instead of a scroll. Soon the churches were in possession of a considerable collection of writings which supplemented the Old Testament Scriptures and recorded the

[3] See above, pp. 25 f.
[4] Was this because the New Testament books, especially the Gospels, started life as private notes?

A page of Codex Sinaiticus (4th century), one of the earliest complete manuscripts of the whole Bible. The 'codex' or notebook form, rather than the scroll, came into common use in the 2nd century, and was adopted from the start for New Testament writings. This page contains John 21:1–25. British Museum, London.

actual words of Christ and the teachings of the immediate circle that surrounded Him.[5]

There was no question as to whether these were authoritative. They were accepted as so without argument. Only with the lapse of time came the question of authenticity. Some

[5] On the history of the Canon, see A. Souter (revised C. S. C. Williams), *The Text and Canon of the New Testament* (Duckworth, 1954). B. M. Metzger, *The Text of the New Testament* (OUP, 1964) has a very good chapter on the production of ancient manuscripts.

people filled in gaps in the stories with romances of their own.[6] Others, with more sinister purposes, tried to palm off their own speculations as apostolic in origin.[7] Discussions over the Canon, or rule, of the New Testament were mainly concerned with ruling out the outsiders that were trying to creep in. Sometimes a picture is painted of a group of clerics, confronted by a heap of books, arbitrarily selecting just a few and declaring these alone to be canonical. Such a view is a travesty of the truth. The question to be settled was largely one of making official what was already general practice. No real questions were ever raised over the Four Gospels, Acts or Paul's letters. Most people were ready to accept the Revelation of John, 1 John, 1 Peter and Hebrews. There was a little hesitation over the acceptance of certain of the smaller New Testament letters (the Syriac-speaking churches were the only notable ones to hesitate; it was not until the fifth century that they dropped their doubts about 2 Peter, 2 and 3 John and Jude), but this was mainly occasioned by the fact that they were seldom read and not often alluded to by earlier writers. A few books had a certain vogue in some churches, but were not allowed to be accounted canonical. However, none of these had wide usage. The *Epistle of Barnabas,* the *Shepherd of Hermas* and the *Didache* might have been admitted in a few congregations. They were now politely relegated to a subordinate position.

Tests for canonical books

What makes a book part of the 'New Testament'? Two main tests were imposed. Did a book come from the time of the apostles? Did it agree with what was already known of apostolic doctrine? Two little incidents illustrate these tests.

The Muratorian Canon[8] is a list of books accepted by the Roman church some time towards the end of the second century. It survives in a Latin copy, which, if original, is about the earliest known Christian document in Latin.[9] It

[6] *E.g.* stories about the childhood of Jesus.
[7] *E.g. Gospel of Thomas,* to further Gnostic ideas.
[8] See Glossary.
[9] Some scholars think it is a very bad translation from a Greek original.

lists the four Gospels, Acts, Paul's letters, the letters of John and Jude and the Revelation of John. There is doubt as to whether it refers to a 'Revelation of Peter' or to a letter of Peter. It expresses doubt over accepting this work, which would probably suit the pseudonymous Revelation better.[1] One oddity is the inclusion of the Wisdom of Solomon, known usually in the Old Testament Apocrypha. Various heretical works which are said to differ greatly from the New Testament doctrines are excluded. The *Shepherd of Hermas*, although popular, is rejected as well, on the grounds that 'it was written very recently, in our times, by Hermas, while his brother Pius was sitting in the chair (*i.e.* was bishop) of the city of Rome'. A popular, and theologically unexceptional, work was ruled out because it did not date from the time of the apostles.

Towards the end of the century, in the little town of Rhossus, close to Antioch, there was trouble.[2] The bishop of Antioch, a certain Serapion, went to investigate. He found that one of the causes of the trouble was a *Gospel of Peter* which was sometimes read in church services. He was prepared to be indulgent until he looked at the actual work. Then it became clear that it was heretical. For one thing, it was suggested that a spirit-power had come down upon the man Jesus, and that it left Him when He was crucified. The cry from the cross was re-written as 'My power, my power, why have you left me?' This did not square with apostolic doctrine. Serapion already knew what the apostles taught from their genuine writings. This work was obviously a forgery put forward to propagate false teaching. It was accordingly banned.

Sometimes it is said that the early Christians were unconcerned about the authenticity of the New Testament documents. It is even stated that they knew that people passed off their own writings as belonging to Paul or Peter. The actual history of the second century refutes this. The writers of historical romances usually had a hard time of it. The book of Acts was the inspiration for several fantasies. While Irenaeus was a young man at Smyrna, one of the church elders there, a

[1] Only a few fragments survive, mainly giving information about the torments of hell in very graphic details.

[2] The incident is recorded in Eusebius, *Church History* vi. 12.

man called Leucius, wrote a fanciful tale about the apostle Paul (it was called the *Acts of Paul*). It was a fairly innocent piece of light fiction, but he was called to account by the church leaders. His plea that he had done it only out of admiration for the apostle met with a frosty reception. He was deposed from his position in the congregation. He is thought to have continued his game of hagiography.[3] The *Acts of John*, the *Acts of Peter* and perhaps certain other romances might be his work. Miracles abound in these tales, together with harrowing accounts of the martyrdom of the apostle concerned, with suitable punishment for the persecutors. Usually they are totally unmemorable, though the odd incident sticks in the memory. The apostle John is depicted as coming to an inn particularly infested with bugs. After a suitable word of command he enters, and passes an undisturbed night. On his departure the next morning, the bugs, lice and other vermin are found lined up on parade outside awaiting the apostle's permission to return to their residence!

Such tales were not the particular trait of Asia Minor alone. Syriac-speaking Christians composed the *Acts of Judas Thomas*, which are the source of the legendary visit of the apostle Thomas to India. Even serious people, such as Justin Martyr, could invent fabulous stories. While in Rome he saw a statue with the inscription 'Semo Sanco Deo' (to the god Semo Sancus). But he misread it as 'Simoni Sancto Deo' (to Simon the holy god), and the story of the battle by magic between Simon Magus and the apostle Peter was born.

The debate over the date of Easter

In some ways it is easier to settle disputes over Christian doctrine when one side is recognizably not Christian. It becomes much more difficult when both sides agree on the main points of the Christian faith but violently disagree on some slightly smaller issue. The second century saw the first disputes where both sides were reasonably true to the main points of apostolic doctrine. The way they tackled their differences is still most instructive.

[3] M. R. James, *The Apocryphal New Testament* (OUP, 1953), gives these romances in full.

From New Testament times, it was accepted that the normal day for Christian worship was Sunday, the Lord's day. Paul preached at the assembly at Troas on the 'first day of the week'.[4] The *Didache*, the *Epistle of Barnabas* and Justin Martyr all provide evidence that Christians met weekly for worship on Sunday, the first day of the week. But year by year they wanted to commemorate the anniversary of Jesus' resurrection. The time of the Passover (the season when Jesus was crucified) was obviously tied to the Jewish calendar. And Passover might fall in mid-week, according to which year it was. Were Christians to keep the Jewish date of Nisan 14 (the fourteenth day of the Jewish month Nisan), or were they to follow normal practice and celebrate the resurrection anniversary on the nearest Sunday?

In general, the various Christian communities observed a Sunday near to the Passover as the anniversary of the resurrection. The congregations of Asia Minor were the main exceptions.[5] They stood firmly for their old practice of having Easter on Nisan 14, whichever day of the week it was. Various groups of churches, from Rome in the west to Osrhoene in the east of Syria, held consultations to settle their practice. These meetings were of delegates from the churches in a particular geographical area. The leaders of the Asia Minor churches found themselves in a minority; Asia Minor had one practice, the rest had another.

The spokesman for the Asia Minor churches was Polycrates, the bishop of the powerful church at Ephesus. He could claim good authority for their custom. His own family included seven 'bishops', all of whom had kept Nisan 14 as Easter. Before them, many outstanding leaders of the churches of Asia Minor had done so. He mentions Melito of Sardis, who wrote a defence of Christianity to the emperor Marcus Aurelius (AD 161–180). Melito was highly respected, and widely travelled (he had even journeyed to Palestine). By a very lucky chance, a sermon of his for the Easter festival has recently been found on a papyrus from Egypt. It shows that the church of Sardis had a leader who was a trained orator as

[4] Acts 20:7.

[5] Eusebius, *Church History* v. 24–25, where the whole dispute is described, and Polycrates's defence of the Asia Minor practice is preserved.

well as a competent expounder of the Scriptures. In his sermon Melito draws direct parallels from the imagery of the Passover to speak of the sufferings of Christ. For Melito, Easter was the Christian Passover; he celebrated it on the Passover date. Polycrates goes on to mention other church leaders, known to us only as names, who kept the Asia Minor practice. Their examples gain extra weight as he states that they died in defence of their Christian faith. Ultimately, he traces the practice of keeping the resurrection anniversary on Nisan 14 to the apostle John himself.

How was this major difference to be settled? Most churches were agreeable to 'live and let live'. But in Rome there were congregations of both persuasions. The bishop of Rome, Victor by name (is there any significance in the fact that he is the first bishop of Rome with a Latin name and not a Greek one?), proclaimed that the Asia Minor communities were banned from Christian fellowship. This took place in about AD 190. But Rome, even with the prestige of Peter and Paul as its founders, was not allowed to get away with this.[6]

Plenty of churches who agreed with Rome in holding Easter on a Sunday were unwilling to condemn their brethren in Asia Minor as heretics, on a trivial point. And they did not like Victor's arrogant and high-handed action. Irenaeus, who had gone from Asia Minor to France, took Victor to task. He pointed out that Victor was departing from the attitude of his predecessors, and he made it perfectly clear that other churches were not going to follow the Roman lead. We do not know whether Victor personally climbed down, or whether his death ended the trouble. Certainly, the Asia Minor churches remained in fellowship, although their peculiar practice gradually died out. The churches then addressed themselves to the almost insoluble problem of which was the correct Sunday for Easter—a problem which has never quite left them!

[6] Peter and Paul were probably martyred in Rome, which gave considerable prestige, and led to the erroneous claim that they had actually founded the church there. For more about authority in the church, see below, pp. 92 ff.

Christian worship in the second century

It is from Justin Martyr that we get the first glimpse of Christian worship after the apostolic age. In his anxiety to refute the allegations of cannibalism, incest and orgies among Christians, he records what happened among the Christian communities that he knew. Since he was born in Samaria, spent some time in Asia Minor, and latterly taught at Rome, his account is probably a good approximation to what happened in most congregations.[7]

Justin describes baptism, and also gives two accounts of the eucharist, the normal form of worship in the Christian congregation week by week. Baptism, when new members were admitted to the church, was normally a prelude to worship. Those who were to be baptized had to undergo a period of instruction. At this time there was no great formality about this, and Justin gives no exact details. At the start of the next century, we are told that three years was considered the regular length of time for instruction before baptism, although it could be shortened for good progress. The teaching given before baptism covered both doctrine and Christian behaviour. Much was made of the forgiveness of sins, and it was expected that both candidate and congregation would fast before the baptism.

The act of baptism took place somewhere other than where the congregation usually met. Perhaps it would be in the local river, or in the adjacent bath-building of the house. Then the

[7] Justin Martyr, *First Apology* 61–65. For more about Justin, see below, pp. 81 ff.

The 'agape' or 'love-feast': two wall-paintings from the Catacomb of Callistus, Rome. Possibly 3rd century AD.

newly-baptized person was brought to the assembled congregation, and all joined in prayer. At the end of the prayers, the congregation greeted each other with a kiss, to show that they were all friends of each other. The kiss was a normal method of greeting for both sexes (as it is to this day in Mediterranean countries), but had a special significance among Christians. When we realize the make-up of the average congregation, where slave and master could be on an equal footing and all distinctions of race and class were forgotten, we can realize something of the significance of the kiss of fellowship. In normal life it would be used between family and friends; here it declared that the variegated congregation was a family! It formed the fitting prelude to the fellowship-meal or eucharist.

Christian worship was very flexible in those days. When there was no baptism (probably on the majority of Sundays), the earlier part of the worship was occupied with Bible readings and preaching. From Justin we gather that ethical matters were the main content of the sermons, but this may well have been meant for outside readers who believed that Christians perpetrated all sorts of unmentionable crimes. One of the church leaders conducted the worship, while another read the Scriptures (the prophets and the Gospels seem to have been most popular). The man in charge was probably the 'bishop', but Justin merely calls him 'the presider'. When the readings and preaching were over, there were the usual prayers, as after a baptism. Whether various people prayed or only one is not clear, but the congregation stood to pray.

After this, the communion service began, although to call it

a separate service is misleading, since it was all part of the normal Sunday worship. A loaf of bread and a cup of wine mixed with water were brought in, and the leader in charge began a long prayer of thanksgiving. It was an extempore prayer, although the subject-matter was probably similar each time. The congregation expressed their assent with a communal 'Amen'. Then other church officials, called 'servants' or 'deacons', distributed the bread and wine to the congregation. Justin says that the bread and wine were called 'thanksgiving' or 'eucharist', and that they were treated as special because of the prayer said over them. Only those who had been baptized were allowed to partake, and there may have been restrictions on those whose personal lives were not up to standard. Justin seems to have held that the bread and wine were in some sense the body and blood of Christ, and ascribes this to the fact that they were sanctified by prayer, but he does not elaborate this. Elsewhere he parallels the eucharist with the sacrifices of the Old Testament (especially the meal-offering). Portions of bread and wine from the communion were taken away at the end of the service for those in need. The service may have ended with more prayer and exhortation.

It is tempting to try and read back later practice into the early days of the church, but it must be resisted. Although Justin might seem in some ways very 'Catholic', in other points the worship he describes would have greater similarity to that of the Brethren today. Alongside the stress on Bible reading and preaching, together with extempore prayer, there is a reverence towards the materials used for communion that could later degenerate into idolatry. Yet even here Justin is not consistent. The communion is still something of a meal, and shares could be taken to those absent. This is not an early case of the 'reserved sacrament', but a practical provision for those who might otherwise go hungry. The 'deacons' were primarily the assistants of the 'overseer/bishop' in serving at the table and administering the poor-relief, and the two tasks were connected. As usual, the early Christians were much concerned with the practicalities of life.

Little has been said so far about church organization, chiefly as there is so little that can be said. Each congregation dealt with its own affairs, although it could receive or ask for advice from another. Originally the older members looked after such simple organization as was needed. They seem to have been elected to their position by the congregation. Gradually one of them would take the lead, and so emerge as the 'overseer/bishop', while others remained as his helpers. Certain members, from an early date, dealt with the poor-relief and other practical needs, and gradually became a recognized order of 'deacons' (some of these could be women). They often came under direct control of the 'bishop', and sometimes one would succeed as 'bishop' when the office became vacant. Church officials held their office for life, and did not usually move from one congregation to another. They were unpaid, except perhaps for small donations in kind, and these gifts seem to have been limited to the 'prophets', who dwindled out of existence during the second century. It seems that church leaders were elected, but we have no certain information. There is no evidence as to how they were formally appointed; perhaps the laying on of hands was used, accompanied with prayer; we just do not know.

The above organization was well suited to the smallish groups of believers in most towns. There might be problems where there was more than one congregation in one town, but one leader usually took charge. He and his council of 'elders' could settle local trouble. Where bigger problems came on the scene, local leaders and delegates could meet to thrash out a difficulty. Although more formalities and a little ceremonial were added as time went on, this kind of arrangement was to prove viable until the churches received the doubtful blessing of state patronage and a sudden influx of adherents.

5

Render to Caesar

The early Christians were faced by a totalitarian state—but their creed taught them that Christ alone deserved unquestioning loyalty. They were prepared to give a lesser allegiance to the civil powers, but not the total obedience and worship which was demanded. How were they to face the inevitable tension and problems? Was it to be outright war with the state? Were they to conform? Or was the answer half-way in between? And if so, how were they to make the state see their point of view?

Religion under the Roman Empire

At present there are two views concerning the relationship between the Roman Empire and the Christians. According to the traditional view, the whole time prior to Constantine was one unmitigated purge against Christianity, carried on with unremitting ferocity. In reaction against this, some recent writers[1] have played down the hostility of the state to the Christians, and have minimized the extent of persecutions, attributing most of them to mob violence rather than official policy. Neither view is wholly correct, but neither is totally wrong.

The attitude of the Roman Empire to religion was peculiar when viewed by modern eyes. On the one hand, there was the state religion, carried out with perfunctory zeal. Alongside, in parallel, were the various cults with their enthusiastic devotees,

[1] *E.g.* W. H. C. Frend, *The Early Church* (Hodder and Stoughton, 1965). For a thorough and balanced survey see A. N. Sherwin-White, *Roman Society and Roman Law in the New Testament* (Oxford University Press, 1963).

cults which satisfied those who needed something satisfying in religion. The state cult required nominal acceptance, but not fervent support. But this nominal acceptance was obligatory! The various other gods were optional, but they could have really fanatical devotees (even if the educated average Roman affected to be above such things).

The position of the emperor made the state cult something of a peculiarity. Although technically 'Pontifex Maximus' (chief priest of the state cult), there was a tendency spreading from the East which would make him a divine being to whom adoration and worship could be directed. Such a trend, however, was not uniform. Some emperors would insist on it, as when Domitian decreed that he should be addressed as 'Our Lord and our God'. Others would ignore it, or even treat it as a joke; on his death-bed, Vespasian could quip, 'I feel I am becoming a god.' In the next century Antoninus Pius was so called because of his unremitting efforts to have Hadrian posthumously deified. Official policy and current practice were out of step. Officially Caesar was not quite worshipped; one could invoke Caesar's 'genius' (the equivalent of his guardian angel!). But the oriental practice of ascribing deity to those whom one would flatter was too strong. Soon a perfunctory acceptance of Caesar's deity would be obligatory.

As far as other cults were concerned, the situation was equally anomalous or tolerant (depending on which point of view you took). A cult might be suppressed on the grounds that it was seditious—this was the excuse for putting down the Druids—but this was unusual. No cult received official acknowledgment of its existence, although an individual emperor might be an enthusiastic devotee. In this hazy situation the Jews had a special position. The trouble was that they were exclusive; other cults could tolerate neighbours, but Yahweh would have no other gods beside Himself. The flexible Romans could arrange a deal with them, however; as long as the Jews offered sacrifice on behalf of the emperor, they could continue their cult. Later emperors took care to regulate what were the privileges of the Jews, and what they could not get away with. There were already signs of the anti-Semitism which would disfigure the Middle Ages, especially after the great Jewish revolt of AD 70. But with a little bending of the rules, even Jews could be included within the imperial scheme. Then came the Christians.

The Roman law and Christianity

At first, as we have seen,[2] Christians were mistaken for Jews. Soon, however, it was recognized that they were different: the Jews saw to that.[3] And once more the Roman imperial

[2] See p. 23.

[3] The expulsion of the Jews from Rome in Claudius's reign was said to be due to rioting instigated by a certain Chrestus (Suetonius, *Life of Claudius* 25. 4; *cf*. Acts 18:2). Was this strife between Jews and Christians?

A household altar to the Lares. The head of each family offered sacrifices to the Lares, spirits taking care of the household, and the Penates, spirits of the storecupboard. From the House of the Vettii, Pompeii.

machine had to deal with an exclusive sect which would not have the gods of this world in any form. 'Sacrifice to Caesar' was the command. It met with stubborn refusal. But although confronted with an apparently seditious movement, the Roman authorities usually refused to hunt them down. In

Deification of a Roman emperor. An ivory panel showing an emperor, possibly Antoninus Pius, being received into heaven. 5th century AD. British Museum, London.

line with the general policy, the state took no cognizance of cults. To the Roman magistrate, the name 'Christian' soon came to mean an enemy of the state. Sedition must be put down, and those who refused to sacrifice to Caesar when so commanded were executed.

Such was the official attitude. But it was coloured by popular rumour. The Christians' secluded meetings, as we saw from Pliny's letter to Trajan,[4] gave rise to rumours of orgies. After all, sexual licence was the rule and not the exception in Roman high society, and ordinary people went to the brothel as readily as to the public baths. Add to this that a pagan might hear Christians calling each other 'brother' or 'sister', and the rumours would increase to those of incest! Incautious references to the body and blood of Christ would suggest cannibalism. And once told, the stories would grow with the telling.

Confronted with a charge of stubborn passive resistance to the state cult, together with added insinuations of secret crimes, one can understand the perplexity of a Roman governor like Pliny. So he punished the 'disloyalty to the state', while trying to investigate the 'crimes'.

From the Christian point of view, this was most unsatisfactory. From the Acts of the Apostles one gets the impression that during Luke's lifetime official policy was to tolerate Christians. But by the opening years of the second century much had changed. A Christian in court would be presumed guilty; plenty of malicious people were ready to forward the charges; respectable people would be alienated because of tales of disgusting behaviour. The record must be put straight.

The Apologists

The writers who tried to put the Christian case are often called the 'Apologists', from the Greek *apologia*, a speech for the defence. In English it is a misleading term, because it implies that they were apologizing for something. They were not. Some of their work was more of a frontal attack on contemporary paganism; much of it was an explanation of what

[4] Above, p. 45.

Christians were and why they were innocent of the charges laid against them. Many of the works written were addressed to the emperor in person. Whether they ever reached him is a moot point, but they certainly had some circulation. But the writers were up against a hard core of public prejudice, and they had to do their task of defending and explaining over and over again.

The first writer of this type whose name we know was a certain Quadratus, who came from Asia Minor. Only one fragment of his work survives,[5] but it is most intriguing. He claims that people healed by Jesus were still alive when he was a young man. Quadratus wrote to the emperor Hadrian, who died in AD 137; if Quadratus was reasonably mature when he wrote, there is no reason to doubt his statement.

[5] Quoted by Eusebius; translation in J. Stevenson, *A New Eusebius*, p. 55.

Bronze head of the emperor Hadrian, found in the Thames at London Bridge. Hadrian was the first Roman emperor to wear a beard. British Museum, London.

Hadrian's villa at Tivoli, near Rome. Hadrian was one of the few emperors who travelled round the Empire. Different parts of his villa at Tivoli were arranged to remind him of places visited; this picture is of the Canopus Pool.

Probably contemporary with Quadratus was an unknown author who wrote the *Letter to Diognetus*. This little work survived until modern times in only one manuscript. Fortunately copies were made, because the original, sole-surviving manuscript was later destroyed by a fire. The *Letter to Diognetus* is in some ways the most appealing work of its kind. The author contrasts Christianity with paganism and Judaism, describing Christians as a third type of mankind. He makes considerable use of the argument from the character of Christians to show the excellence of their faith. He points out how Christians do not indulge in many evil practices then current, such as exposing unwanted babies on the local rubbish-dump. Christians are commended as a preservative in society and their virtue reminds other men that they cannot find true fulfilment by their own efforts.

Under Antoninus Pius and Marcus Aurelius, the Roman

emperors who followed Hadrian, the 'Apologists' flourished. Many who wrote were men with some philosophical training, such as Aristides and Justin Martyr. Aristides came from Athens, but we know little of him, or of his fellow-Athenian Athenagoras, who wrote both an apology and a treatise on the resurrection of the body. The usual line of attack was to refute the charges of incest and cannibalism, and to follow it up with a critique of contemporary ideas of the gods, with suitable condemnation of the Olympian deities and their human devotees. The treatise would close with an appeal to the excellence of the Christian idea of the unity of God, with perhaps some reference to Jesus as God's final revelation. A generous amount of space might be devoted to showing what Christians were really like, and to arguing the superiority of monotheism.

Justin Martyr

Most of the Apologists were men who had some knowledge of contemporary philosophy, and generally they had more than a little sympathy with it. Plato, especially, was favoured, because his idea of an 'ultimate good' to be contemplated could be used to point the way to the one true God. Justin Martyr is in many ways typical of the philosopher-turned-Christian who wanted to commend his new-found faith.

He had been born of pagan parents in Samaria, and had been something of a professional student. He had done the rounds of most philosophical teachers, sampling their ideas. He found most to be very shallow, and only interested in the fee that they would collect. After searching round, he had chosen Platonism as the philosophy he found most congenial. At this point he happened to visit Ephesus. There he went for a walk by the sea, and met an old man. The two of them talked about how God could be known, and about the nature of the soul. All Justin's answers were insufficient, and so the old man suggested that Justin should base his philosophy on God's revelation in the Hebrew Scriptures with their fulfilment in Jesus. After the old man had left him, Justin says that it seemed as if a fire had been kindled in him. He immediately devoted himself to his new line of study. From then onwards

Ephesus, one of the major cities of the Empire, where Justin Martyr was converted to Christianity.

he was a *Christian* philosopher, and later when he settled at Rome he gave lessons in his house. Justin himself tells the story of his conversion during a debate that he had with a Jew called Trypho (perhaps the famous Rabbi Tarphon who narrowly escaped death when involved in the last Jewish revolt of Bar Cochba in AD 135). This dialogue, and the two apologies, make up the sum of Justin's surviving writings.

In his Apology, Justin takes the normal lines of attack, with especial stress on the good behaviour of the Christians and the messianic prophecies of the Old Testament. He claims that all that is good in pagan philosophy has been borrowed from the Hebrew Scriptures! To Justin, conversion was mainly an ethical and rational thing, concerned with a change of attitude and behaviour. It was given authority and content by appeal to the Scriptures. As a refutation of rumours of orgies, Justin gives the description of Christian worship, which we noted earlier.

Justin and the later Apologists were the first to try to explain the relationship of Christ to God the Father. The question that they must have met was how could Christ be God if there was only One God. In answer, they used the concept of the 'Word' of God (from the prologue to John's Gospel), meaning God's Mind or Reason. This, they held, was present in a small way in human beings, but was seen in its fullness in Jesus. He had first become visible as God's 'Word' at the creation of the world, and when on earth He was God's Wisdom in human form. The main criticism of such a view is that it could make Jesus no more than the best of human beings; but it was a reasonable attempt to see Jesus as a real Mediator between God and man.

Justin had written his *First Apology* at his leisure. The *Second Apology* is much shorter, and was rushed off after three Christians at Rome had been executed on the sole ground of their faith. It gives us a tiny picture of what being a Christian might mean in second-century Rome. A woman of loose morals, married to a man of similar behaviour, was converted. Her husband could not stand her change of life, and made her life a misery. She contemplated a separation, but refrained from actually seeking one. Then her husband tried to get her into court. For a variety of reasons he failed to bring a case against her, and so he turned his anger on the pastor of the Christian congregation where his wife worshipped. The pastor was dragged into court, and was asked if he was a Christian. He replied 'Yes', and was immediately condemned to death. A man in court protested at the procedure, and was found to be a Christian too. He shared the pastor's fate, as did another who was seized at the same time.

Justin might well protest. He might even point to a decree from the emperor Hadrian which said that Christians were to be punished only for specific crimes. The same judge whose procedure Justin had attacked was soon to have Justin himself in the dock (AD 165). It is said that Justin was charged by a rival philosopher who was aggrieved at Justin's success as a teacher. Whether this was true or not, several other Christians were arrested with Justin, and they were hauled to court together.[6] It was clear from the start that the judge was looking

[6]The account of the trial is translated in J. Stevenson, *A New Eusebius*, pp. 28–30.

for a capital charge. They were commanded to sacrifice to the state gods. They refused. The judge, the city prefect Rusticus, was something of a bully. He contemptuously questioned Justin over his beliefs, but it was all a show. After he could get no more information about the organization of the Christians, he came to the point. He asked each of the accused if they were Christians. They admitted that they were. Some were children of Christian parents; others had been taught by Justin; one had come as a slave from Phrygia in Asia Minor; another came from Cappadocia, further east. They may not have been very clever, but they did not waver. Rusticus threatened them with flogging and execution. Jeering, he asked Justin if he thought he would ascend to heaven. 'I don't *think* so', replied Justin. 'I know and am fully convinced of it.' After one last fruitless effort to get them to sacrifice to the state gods, Rusticus condemned them to death. It was thus that Justin received the surname of Martyr.

Not all the 'Apologists' were ready to take a conciliatory line towards Greek philosophy. One bishop of Antioch, named Theophilus, devoted much of three books written to a pagan friend Autolycus to an attack on the immoral pagan myths. Apart from the fact that he is the first writer to use the term 'triad' or 'trinity' to describe the Godhead, however, his claim to fame is small.

A better writer of invective was the Syrian Tatian, author of the *Diatessaron*.[7] Tatian agreed with other Apologists that Greek philosophy had borrowed from the Hebrew Scriptures, but he took a different line when he evaluated it. Perhaps the virulence of his attack is a reaction against the debased and immoral cults which flourished in his native Syria. He learned nothing from Justin Martyr, his old teacher, about conciliation towards the best of pagan philosophy. All was condemned. Everything that was not Christian was totally evil, and the result of demonic forces. Tatian had neither the concern nor patience with the world as he found it. With savage delight he catalogues the immoral statues of Rome, and pronounces doom on all the works of paganism. Nice light reading for Tatian's friends; but how far would this convince his pagan audience?

[7] See above, p. 56.

Pagan views of Christians

The battle of words was not one-sided. Pagans were ready to strike back at Christians. On the purely literary front, they did little. Fronto, the learned tutor of Marcus Aurelius, the philosopher-emperor, is said to have attacked Christians in a public speech. It seems that he merely repeated the usual charges of atheism and immorality. A much more witty attack came from the satirist Lucian of Samosata. Lucian was a man of few beliefs, dedicated to the work of debunking the faith of others. He was also the first person to write space-fiction! (His astronauts sailed up to the moon up a moon-beam.) Lucian tells us the story of Proteus Peregrinus, a wandering magician and lecturer in philosophy, and how for a while he joined the Christians. Lucian pokes fun at the simple Christians, who were taken in by such a charlatan as Proteus. He mentions how they loyally visited Proteus when he was in jail, and did all sorts of things for him. Eventually, according to his tale, Proteus was excommunicated for some breach of discipline. The satirical attack, however, does show how Christians were renowned, even by outsiders, for their hospitality and caring for each other.

While Irenaeus was trying to patch up the churches in France, a formidable attack on Christianity was launched by a writer called Celsus. This attack (one of the few carefully-constructed literary attacks on Christianity) was dangerous because it was carried out by a man who had studied his subject. It was fifty years before there was a Christian sufficiently educated to refute it. (It is from Origen's refutation that we know the work.) Again, the hostile witness gives some interesting views of Christians. To him they were mainly uneducated people, such as weavers, cobblers, laundry-workers and farm labourers. But their zeal in spreading the faith was unbounded. Celsus complains that one had only to look the other way for Christians to turn up and try to spread their propaganda. As many a rationalist has done since, Celsus hits out at the emphasis on faith. But it is obvious from Celsus' remarks that Christian witnessing was both widespread and effective. The Christians that Celsus had met had spoken much of Jesus and His suffering on the cross, for Celsus derides the Christian devotion to the 'crucified sophist'.[8] Surprisingly, Celsus does not deny Jesus' miracles; instead he tries to relegate them to the level of conjuring tricks done at fairs. The virgin birth and the resurrection come in for rough treatment, as does the whole idea of the incarnation of God's Son. In the philosophical climate then current, the idea that the exalted Supreme Being of the universe had become entangled with the evil material world was the rankest heresy. But Celsus' sneers show that he took the challenge of Christianity seriously. He was not alone in this. The emperor at this time was Marcus Aurelius. He was no friend of the Christians, yet even he had to admit that the Christians' fortitude in face of death was similar to that which the 'true philosopher' ought to show.

Persecution in the late second century

The sneers of Lucian and the logic of Celsus were unusual in that age. The general public had a quick and easy way with Christians. With the court procedure loaded against the Christians, and with the amphitheatres needing fodder to appease the blood-lust of the crowd, the situation was simple. As Tertullian put it, 'If the Tiber reaches the walls, if the Nile does not rise to the fields, if the sky doesn't move or the earth does, if there is famine, if there is plague, the cry is at once, "Christians to the lion!" What, all of them to one lion?'

The Romans had not always been as bestial as they were in the later years of the Empire. Execution for Roman citizens was usually beheading with a sword. Non-Romans might expect to be crucified, especially if they were slaves. Throwing prisoners to wild beasts was a novel punishment. It had first taken place by accident, in the reign of Augustus, when a noted brigand had been kept in a cage prior to his appearance in the arena in a gladiatorial show. Under that cage there had been a cage full of starving lions, kept ready for the wild-beast hunt which was to follow the gladiators. The handiwork of the stage carpenters had been poor, and the upper cage collapsed. The bandit fell down among the lions and was torn to pieces.

[8] *Cf.* the famous graffito from the ruins on the Palatine Hill at Rome, where a man is depicted worshipping a crucified figure with an ass's head.

Roman 'bestiari' fighting lions. The 'bestiari' were men who fought beasts, as opposed to gladiators, who fought each other. Terra cotta relief from the Museo delle Terme, Rome.

The crowd saw it and liked it; the next time it happened it was done on purpose. The Roman crowds were already accustomed to seeing men fight to the death in gladiatorial contests; they were blood-hungry. Soon no public spectacle was complete without throwing some criminals to the wild beasts, with or without public torture as well.

Christians lived under constant threat of the storm breaking. In 177 persecution broke out in France, and many members of the congregations at Lyons and Vienne were seized. The subsequent story of their fate is told in a letter which the survivors sent back to their friends in Asia Minor.[9]

The trouble started with the mob. Christians were attacked and harassed. Their homes were raided and they were beaten and some were put in prison. The governor of the province was ready to gratify the worst desires of the mob. The first group of prisoners were tortured and condemned. One man

[9] In Eusebius, *Church History* v. 1. 3–63.

tried to act as advocate for the Christians, apparently trying to refute allegations of secret crimes. He was seized, and when he admitted that he was a Christian, he was sentenced to death as well. In prison, some broke down under the strain of beatings and torture. But recantations did not bring them release. By now a witch-hunt was in full cry. Most of the prominent members of the two congregations were arrested. Slaves of the accused were tortured in order to get 'evidence' of 'crimes'.[1] Torture was increased.

Among those tortured was a slave-girl called Blandina. She and her mistress were both Christians, but some feared that

[1] This was normal Roman court procedure.

Roman bronze helmet, from Hawkedon, Suffolk. The weight of the helmet and width of the neck-band suggest that it was used in gladiatorial fights. If so, it is the only piece of gladiatorial armour to be found in Britain. 1st century AD. British Museum, London.

88

the young girl would not stand firm. The soldiers wore themselves out in an attempt to break her, but they failed. They tortured one of the church officials from Vienne, a deacon called Sanctus, but he seemed miraculously able to withstand the torments (these included applying red-hot plates of brass to the most tender parts of his body).

After torture, the prisoners were thrown back into the prison, a stinking hole, dark and filthy. Many died there from suffocation. Yet others were arrested, and were flung in in place of the dead. Old Pothinus, the bishop of the Lyons congregation, was over 90 when arrested. His age did not save him from being beaten up by the governor's soldiers, but he died in jail before they could torture him.

In the end all the prisoners seem to have been taken to the amphitheatre. Those who had been weak at first took courage and reaffirmed their faith in Christ. Then the sickening game began. Some, including Blandina, were thrown to the beasts. Most died, but Blandina survived for another day of torture. Those who were found to be Roman citizens were reserved for execution by beheading. A letter came from the emperor (Marcus Aurelius) saying that those who persisted in their Christian profession should be tortured to death. As there was a big festival at Lyons, it seemed to the governor that this was just the right time. While the Christians were being publicly tortured, a local doctor (a Christian of Asiatic origin) was seen to encourage them not to deny Christ. He was arrested and thrown to the wild beasts. In the end only Blandina and a fifteen-year-old lad called Ponticus were left alive. The rest had been torn and battered to death or had been burned alive. Ponticus died under torture, refusing to deny Christ. Blandina was battered senseless by a wild bull, and finally died. The fantastic courage of this young girl amazed even hardened pagans. This was the sort of thing they could neither understand nor forget. As a futile last gesture the corpses of the martyrs were kept for six days under guard, without burial. After this they were burned and the ashes were thrown into the river Rhône. The Romans thought that they could prevent the resurrection by such an action.

The martyrs of Vienne and Lyons live on, their names remembered in history. But it is only a coincidence that we know of them. There were no doubt many other martyrs who suffered similar fates in other places who are now unknown. From the limited evidence that survives we cannot make a comprehensive list of all persecutions, let alone all martyrs. Those who were faithful to Christ even in face of a barbaric and excruciating death were, for the most part, obscure people, with little of education or social status to commend them. To the pagan crowds that watched them die, they were a contemptible though stubborn sect. To the authorities they were an

A bust of the philosopher-emperor Marcus Aurelius, who was emperor at the time of the persecution at Lyons and Vienne. Museo Capitolino, Rome.

inexplicable enigma, refusing to conform. Yet they could not explain how it was that a crucified Jesus could inspire such loyalty, which made even young girls defy torture that would have broken most men. The Roman Empire acted with unreasoning fear, and struck with unbelievable savagery. But in the little groups of Christians, the martyrs were venerated as the top-ranking Christians. Even after the persecutions were ended, for a long while it was virtually impossible for someone to be reckoned a saint unless they had been martyred.[2] The values of Rome were turned upside-down, and those who died in the arena, refusing to deny Christ, were accorded the highest rank. The anniversaries of their deaths, often paradoxically called their 'birthdays', were to become almost as great festivals as Easter. The tedious lists of saints in mediaeval calendars and litanies started as the roll-call of the martyrs. And it was a roll-call which was the glory of the churches.

[2] The first non-martyr who was widely regarded as a saint was Martin of Tours (c. AD 316–397).

6

Wider still and wider

No organization can live on its initial enthusiasm for ever. The church born in the white heat of revival will be succeeded by a second generation where the initial gains are consolidated. If it is to last beyond another generation, there must be organization and planning. The enthusiasm of the apostolic age gave way to the calmer, less excitable faith of the early second century. When it became obvious that Christ was not returning in the immediate future, plans had to be made in case He delayed His coming still further. Pressing problems of the day could no longer be left. And people gifted to organize the churches as lasting institutions were needed. At the same time, the centre of gravity of Christianity shifted. Asia Minor declined in importance, while Rome and Alexandria became prominent. Christians appear in new areas for the first time, and these new advances needed consolidation with help from longer-established Christians.

Authority in the church

Contemporary with Irenaeus was Dionysius, the bishop of the church at Corinth. He was a great letter-writer; although none of his voluminous correspondence survives verbatim (except for a few small fragments), Eusebius gives us an idea of his interests. We find the bishop of Corinth writing not only to Christians in Sparta and Athens, but to those as far afield as Gortyna in Crete, Amastris in northern Asia Minor, and Rome. Such letters were read out at church worship, perhaps

The ancient town of Corinth, dominated by the Temple of Apollo.

providing additional sermons otherwise unavailable before the twentieth-century invention of the tape-recorder.

Dionysius was concerned with doctrine, for he expressly attacked the heretic Marcion in one of his letters, and several other letters are said to contain more general exhortations to orthodoxy of belief. But practical matters of conduct also take a considerable part. He had to pick up the pieces when the congregation at Athens almost disbanded under persecution (their bishop had been one of the victims). Perhaps it was a similar situation to that which Irenaeus was facing at Lyons after the persecution of AD 177. Marriage and chastity were dealt with in another letter; and there was the problem of members falling away as well. Dionysius seems to have been a humane man, counselling leniency to the fallen if they wanted to return to the congregation, and telling one bishop not to pitch his demands in matters of conduct too high.

Dionysius is of importance as being a very average church leader. The fact that he could write to widely separated groups is evidence of good communication between the churches. Irenaeus's own ability to link Asia Minor, Rome and France is similar evidence. The churches were not merely living for themselves; they took notice of what was happening elsewhere, and would even go and help if the matter was urgent. But 'help' and 'advice' might well be construed as interference, as the Roman church found out when its leader Victor tried to interfere over the date of Easter as observed in Asia Minor.[1] Local churches, or at least groups of churches, held on to their own independence. Power to advise was still strictly vested in the man, not the office. Irenaeus or Dionysius of Corinth pronounced on various matters with an authority based on their personal wisdom, and holiness of life, not because they held a certain official position. It was perhaps inevitable that eventually a church with a succession of strong leaders might gain the leadership in an area, but such a development was still in the future.

Legal formulations, by which a certain church had authority over a particular area, first appear in the fourth century. The canons of the Council of Nicaea (AD 325) recognize Alexandria, Rome and Antioch as having a certain authority in the regions

[1] See above, pp. 67 ff.

around them, and it is decreed that synods shall meet in each of the civil provinces twice a year. The church of Rome was granted certain powers to hear appeals at the Council of Sardica (AD 342), but this council was not representative of the Eastern churches, and the powers may have been given only in order to give a semblance of legality to the support which the Western churches were then giving to Athanasius (he had been deposed from his post as bishop of Alexandria, and had appealed to the Western churches for reinstatement). All these concern matters of law and order, and not doctrine. Legal acknowledgment of the church of Rome as the proper place for appeals from church courts was given by the emperor Gratian in AD 378. The claim of Rome to exercise jurisdiction was at first based on the association of the apostles Peter and Paul with the early history of the church. Later, at the end of the fourth century, in the time of bishop Damasus, considerable use began to be made of the famous text in Matthew 16:18. With the collapse of the Western Empire, the church at Rome became one of the great civil institutions of Western Europe, and from then on one can justifiably talk of Roman primacy in matters of law and doctrine.

In the second century there was no such primacy, but because Rome was the metropolis, the church there gained a certain amount of prestige. This was increased by the fact that it claimed two apostles as its founders, Peter and Paul. The fact that they were both martyrs enhanced the claim. But it was a long time before the church at Rome had a really outstanding leader. The great men of the second century in Rome, whether orthodox or heretical, were all immigrants. Rome jealously treasured its list of leaders from the apostles onwards; such a list was probably shown to Hegesippus, a Jewish Christian who visited Rome about AD 180, and who collected reminiscences about the apostles. It is to Hegesippus that we owe most of our information about the death of James the Lord's brother, and a strange tale of how two grandsons of Jude, the Lord's brother, were summoned before the emperor Domitian and questioned about the kingdom of Christ. Apparently, on hearing that the kingdom was to come at the end of time, and seeing that they were just poor farmers, the emperor dismissed them unharmed.[2]

Rome was to be torn with dissension in the early years of the third century, but the church survived to become great. This is perhaps due to the resurgence of the Latin language, and to the fact that Rome suddenly found itself as the only apostolic foundation in the Latin-speaking sector. Until Victor, in the last years of the second century, all the Roman bishops had Greek names. It was from North Africa that Latin returned to Rome, after an eclipse of nearly a century.

The resurgence of Latin

Greek had been a lingua franca in the Near East ever since the conquests of Alexander the Great (died 323 BC). With the Roman expansion eastward, the Greek culture entered Rome like a flood. Latin literature had its greatest flowering in the last days of the Republic and in the reign of the first emperor, Augustus (Jesus was born during his reign; Augustus was ultimately responsible for the census which took Joseph and Mary to Bethlehem). The latter part of the first century AD is often called the Silver Age of Latin. It reached its climax, and its point of eclipse, around the end of that century. The historian Tacitus and the satirist Juvenal are the last great

[2] See Eusebius, *Church History* ii. 23; iii. 20.

The Forum, Rome, centre of the Roman Empire until the 4th century, when the Empire split into Eastern and Western parts. The Colosseum is in the background. The emperors' palaces were situated off on the right.

Latin authors of the old classical tradition. Juvenal had bemoaned the fact that Rome was becoming a Greek city. The Latin of Petronius is heavy with Greek loan-words. The second century saw Juvenal's worst fears confirmed. The emperor Hadrian wrote mainly in Greek, though his little ode to his soul is in Latin. Marcus Aurelius wrote his *Meditations* in Greek, though he could write letters to his tutor Fronto in Latin. When the Apologists wrote to the emperors, explaining the Christian faith, they too wrote in Greek. The Latin language took refuge in North Africa, where its pagan resurgence came with writers like Apuleius.[3] It is from North Africa, too, that we have our first Christian writings in Latin.

The beginnings of Christianity in North Africa

The town of Scilli was so unimportant that we cannot be sure where it was; but this obscure little place provides us with our first-known event of Latin-speaking Christianity. The fact that Christians had penetrated to such an out-of-the-way place presupposes that they were already well established in the larger cities of North Africa.

Six Christians from Scilli were brought before the governor at Carthage.[4] It was 17 July AD 180. They were the second group of six to be brought for trial. There were no great speakers among them, and to the onlookers they must have seemed a group of poor, inarticulate but stubborn people. Four were women; the remainder were men. The governor thought to argue them back to normal (as he saw it) practice, but he met with point-blank refusal when he demanded that they sacrifice to the state gods. The prisoners protested that they were peaceable folk, innocent of any crime, but determined to follow the truth. Their spokesman, a certain Speratus, held firmly to his allegiance to the Lord of the universe. In his possession were the Old Testament, and Paul's letters; he seems to have brought them to the trial, perhaps in a naïve hope that when the governor read them he

[3] He wrote a novel called *The Golden Ass* (c. AD 114–c. 185), a work noted mainly for its pornographic leanings and its exaltation of the mysteries of Isis.
[4] English translation of the incident in J. Stevenson, *A New Eusebius*, pp. 41–43.

Map 3

The Western Area

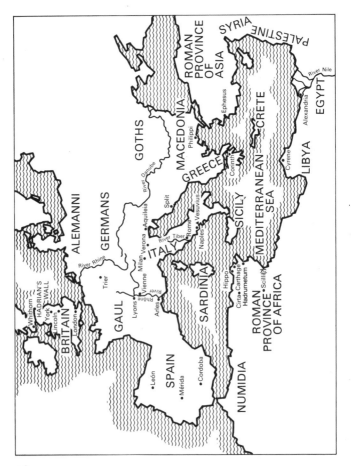

would be convinced that Christians were innocent and would acquit them.

The governor tried to persuade them; he even offered a month's stay of execution as time for repentance. He might have spared his breath. The Christians from Scilli may have been uneducated, but their loyalty to Christ was unflinching. When it was proclaimed that they should be beheaded, they all said, 'Thanks be to God!' They were the first in a long line of martyrs from North Africa.

In many ways the martyrs of Scilli were typical of North African Christianity. Their faith was hard and unyielding, but with more emotion than intellectual basis. Their churches were the 'churches of the martyrs', and martyrdom was counted the highest honour that anyone could have. Even to have suffered in persecution was reckoned a high honour. Fifty years later, we read of a Christian who was left for dead after an anti-Christian riot. He recovered, and rejoined his congregation, and was automatically appointed 'presbyter' (church elder) because of his suffering for Christ. And this was no isolated example.

Coupled with the high opinion of martyrs was a resolute intolerance of laxity and of interfering authority. This was to split the churches of North Africa in the fourth century, when a great dispute broke out over what was to be done with those who had weakened under persecution. But to the simple mind of Christians like those of Scilli, the issue was plain. They were soldiers in God's army. Those who denied Him in persecution were no better than deserters! Even when the imperial authorities were tolerant of Christianity, in the time of Constantine and after, the North African churches kept up this embattled idea of Christianity. Perhaps they were wiser than they knew, when they said that the devil had merely changed his tactics in getting the emperor to tolerate Christianity. But it could be said with fairness that some North African Christians would render very little to Caesar at all, and even that with a very bad grace!

Since North African Christianity viewed itself as on a wartime footing, it often generated more heat than light. While it did have its great theologians (such as Tertullian, Cyprian, Tyconius and Augustine), the rank and file were not very literate theologically. The Bible was never translated into the native vernacular of Numidia and Tunisia, as had been done in Egypt. And those who spoke Latin well were probably not a majority. The great strength of North African Christianity (and especially its Donatist section) was among the Punic-speaking inhabitants. But these people never had the Bible in their own language, and perhaps this accounts for the fact that when the Muslim invasions came in the seventh century, North African Christianity was swept away without trace.[5] In earlier years its theologians were not over-ready to debate Christianity with contemporary culture; their attitude was one of a truceless war! The result was a certain shallowness, but it also resulted in a zeal which in its day was without equal. The North African Christians certainly grasped the basic truth that one did not have to be an intellectual to come to Christ. Yet they often failed to learn that one needed more than martyrs and defiance to commend the faith.

Tertullian

Typical of North African Christianity is its first great writer, Tertullian. He is the first great Christian in the early history of the church whom succeeding ages would not canonize but dare not condemn. Tertullian was a pagan lawyer, born in Carthage, and educated in both Greek and Latin. Some of his work as a lawyer still survives in Roman legal collections. He was converted when nearly forty, and immediately turned his considerable rhetorical skill in defence of his new-found faith. He was the stuff of which martyrs were made, but in spite of his voluminous writings and his hard-line attack on so many points (not to mention his searing attacks on Roman officialdom), he seems to have survived to an advanced age and died peacefully. He was married, and one can have sympathy with his poor wife who was probably subjected to a daily oration from her husband.

Later in his life he joined the Montanists, who had spread

[5] Another factor in the complete eradication of Christianity from North Africa is that after the collapse of the Roman Empire in the West, North Africa was taken over by the Vandals, who upheld Arianism (see Glossary) and persecuted orthodox Christians.

The Roman town of Cyrene, in the province of Cyrenaica. The Roman period was a golden age for the North African towns; the remains of Cyrene and of Leptis Magna in Tripolitania are a good indication of the prosperity of these ports. Sabellius probably came from Cyrene.

to North Africa. From this vantage-point he scourged the remainder of the churches for their sins (real and imagined). It is said that in his last years he left the Montanists and founded his own sect. The Tertullianists survived as a distinct group until the fourth century, when they were re-admitted into fellowship with mainstream Christianity, as their particular opinions were not considered heretical enough to exclude them.

The debt of Western Christianity to Tertullian is incalculable, because he gave it a theological language and set of terms. Words like 'sacrament', 'resurrection', 'substance', 'person' (used in discussions on the Trinity), and 'penitence' were all selected by Tertullian as theological terms. The very name 'New Testament' was coined by him. But Tertullian also gave Latin a new lease of life. He begins where Tacitus leaves off. Just a century before, Tacitus had written his historical works, drawing considerably on the rhetorical training that he had received. Tacitus's history was written to be declaimed, and brilliant epigrams abound. In Tertullian they come almost every sentence! Tertullian also carries on Tacitus's compressed style, which makes him hard to read in the original and leaves the translator struggling to keep the original's pungent force. But, above all, Tertullian is an advocate. Whether it is putting contemporary paganism in the dock, or cross-examining some heretic in the witness-box of his mind, Tertullian is brilliant. He has all the hot-blooded emotions at his command. At times he may shout hard because his argument is a bit weak, but he is striving for a favourable verdict all the time.

Tertullian's writings

Thirty-one of Tertullian's writings survive, falling into three categories—apologetic, doctrinal and practical. As a lawyer, his apologetic works are probably his greatest. He tears the Roman legal procedure to shreds, pointing out its glaring inconsistencies when dealing with Christians. He demands why Christians alone are not allowed to speak in their own defence. He questions the reasoning of judges who torture other suspects to obtain the truth, but torture Christians to obtain a denial. But Tertullian is not a man to confine himself to legal points. He refutes the allegations of 'secret crimes' by describing Christian meetings; yet even here he cannot miss a chance for a sly dig at Roman officialdom. He remarks, in an aside, that Christian church leaders are appointed because of their merit, not because (as with pagan priesthoods) they have paid for the honour!

The worship Tertullian describes is both dignified and relaxed. People come to the meeting, making a contribution to the common fund for poor-relief. The meal (Tertullian says it was called by the Greek word for 'love', 'agape') was simple, and the eating and drinking decorous. After this simple communion, still in the setting of a meal, the rest of the time is spent in reading the Bible aloud or in solo singing in praise of God, and the evening concludes with prayer. Prayer is practical and extempore; and Tertullian takes pains to point out that even the emperor and government are commended to God in prayer. So much for charges of sedition!

One feels most sympathy with Tertullian the apologist. Tertullian the doctrinal writer excites less sympathy, and some of his ideas are vaguely horrifying. He uses every weapon in his barrister's armoury. He attacks heretics with a preliminary objection that they have no right to make use of the Scriptures. But this is not his only line of attack. He aims to refute them at every step of their argument, wanting to win every way—rather like the man facing a charge of defamatory language, who swore that he didn't say it, but that if he did it was privileged conversation, and anyway it was true! Tertullian's argument was dangerous. It was true that the apostolic church had the right to claim to be God's true spokesman, but such arguments would later play into the hands of those who wanted a church supreme and beyond the judgment of Scripture. But Tertullian was not thinking of that. Anyway, he had much more ammunition to fire off against the heretics. He deals with Marcion by a mixture of shrewd argument and vicious invective, and he also turns his attention to various Gnostics.

His treatise on baptism is valuable because it is the only full-length treatment from the first three centuries of church history. But once again Tertullian treads on dangerous ground. To him, baptism is a rite of terrific potency. The rite, and especially the water, has power to cleanse from all sin, thanks to the power of God whose name is invoked over it. A fair argument, when one is arguing against the false magic of pagan rites, but horribly dangerous in that it opens the way to all sorts of superstition. Tertullian was well aware of the superstition attached to baptism, for he censures those who would have children baptized. But he was cutting the ground from under his own feet. In time, baptismal superstition would mean that not only babies but even corpses could be baptized.[6]

Tertullian argued rather better when he dealt with the doctrine of the Trinity. His opponent, a certain Praxeas, was sufficiently close to the biblical data to make everyone think hard, and Tertullian comes to grips with the whole problem. The basic dilemma in all Trinitarian doctrine is just this. The Father is God, the Son is God, the Holy Spirit is God, yet there are not three Gods but one. Praxeas and some of his Roman colleagues stressed the unity of God to such an extent that they could say that the Father was crucified! The names of Father, Son and Spirit were treated as interchangeable names for the one God. Now this obviously makes nonsense of Christ's talking to His Father in the New Testament, not to mention other problems.

Tertullian is swift to attack in reply. He uses the concept of the 'Word' of God, as found in John's Gospel, to explain the difference between Father and Son. In his work he coined the word *trinitas* (Latin for Trinity), and explains the Trinity in terms of an expansion of God to deal with the work of the incarnation. Tertullian strives hard to make the distinction of the three Persons, in so doing giving the word 'person' much of its present meaning. (Formerly it could mean a mask for an actor, or a legal term for a holder of property.) From our vantage-point, so much later on, we can see Tertullian's weak points—there is, for instance, the problem of Christ's pre-existence before the incarnation—but even so, his solution is a fine effort for a man attacking the problem from scratch. All later Latin theology depends on his pioneer work.

Tertullian's practical tracts have little real value in themselves, as they are often opinionated and arrogant. But they do shed light on the church life of those days. Colloquial Greek was still much used in worship. Tertullian cites 'for ever and ever' as a phrase used in prayer in Greek; but the same phrase was not necessarily liturgical. It could also be used to praise a gladiator! Tertullian indignantly asks how one could use such a phrase to praise the bestial acts of the gladiatorial shows when one also used it to praise God. Evidently he did not find the equivalent of 'Ee-ay-addio!' from the Kop crowd out of

[6] The practice of baptizing corpses (and of giving communion to the dead!) is condemned in a decree of the Council of Carthage of AD 397.

place in Christian praise; he would only have objected to singing 'O worship the King' in praise of a football star!

He wrote other tracts, such as the one on prayer, where he gives a commentary on the Lord's Prayer; or one on repentance, where he deals with the question of the judgment meted out to those church members who sin badly after baptism. Later on, Tertullian was to make a distinction between forgivable and unforgivable sins. He also retracted his earlier views over forgiveness by the congregation. He attacks the claim made by some church dignitary to forgive all sins after due penance, and also has some harsh things to say about the church not being a 'covey of bishops'. Even Tertullian had to do some explaining on his own account from time to time. He was criticized for dressing in the cloak worn by teachers of philosophy. He gives a spirited defence, but incidentally shows that Christian leaders were not expected to adopt distinctive forms of dress.

Tertullian's works show clearly the way which North African Christianity would take, a way of enthusiasm, martyrdom and heated controversy. But it was a way with its own particular attractiveness, as the report of an incident contemporary with Tertullian shows.

The martyrdom of Perpetua and Felicitas

Tertullian may well have been responsible for editing an account of the martyrdom of some Christians in Carthage in about AD 202. It is an unusual account, in that part of the work is written by the actual martyrs themselves. Vibia Perpetua begins the story. She was twenty-two, married, and had a baby boy. She was arrested, along with two slaves and two others. Subsequently another Christian man joined them in prison. Her father was very much against her, and she had only recently been baptized when she was arrested. Two church officials bribed the authorities so that Perpetua could have her baby with her. Perpetua's brother was able to see her, and she told him of a vision she had had: she saw one of the other prisoners ascend a ladder, defying a dragon; he then invited her to follow, and she climbed to the top where she met the

105

Good Shepherd Himself. She says that as a result of the vision she knew she must die.

They were hauled before the governor, but not before Perpetua's father had changed his threats to pleas, in an attempt to make her renounce Christ. Her baby was taken from her. The day of the 'games', when they were to die, drew near. Her father went frantic with worry. Perpetua herself tells of other visions which she had, and how they encouraged her, but there were other problems in the prison. Felicitas, a slave-girl arrested with Perpetua, was eight months pregnant. In prison she gave birth to a baby girl, who was whisked away and adopted by the Christians. All the while there was harassment to be endured from the prison guards, but we are informed that the treatment improved after the conversion of the prison governor!

The narrator takes up the tale on the day of the martyrdom. One of the prisoners had died in jail. The remainder were

The 'Good Shepherd' theme in art was a favourite one for the early Christians. (1) A sarcophagus from the Museo Cristiano Lateranense, Rome, has three figures of the Good Shepherd. (2) A painting from the ceiling of one of the rooms in the Catacomb of Domitilla, Rome.

thrown to the beasts, as the climax to the spectacle in the amphitheatre. The animals had been starved and goaded to make them furious, and one of the amphitheatre attendants was killed while trying to tie one of the Christians to a wild boar. The bloodthirsty crowd waited expectantly. Perpetua and Felicitas held hands as they faced the beasts—the young girl of noble family and the slave-girl together. Their courage amazed everyone. They were horribly battered, but the beasts did not kill them, and they had to be finished off by the public executioner. Another Christian dipped a ring in his own blood as he was about to die, and handed it to a soldier who seems to have been a secret believer. The effect on the crowd was stunning. Even the executioner's hand shook as he killed the victims. Tertullian was right when he said that the blood of martyrs is the seed of the church.

Leptis Magna, in the Roman province of Tripolitania. The Basilica (bottom of picture) and Forum (just above) were built by Septimius Severus, *c.* 200, round about the time when Perpetua and Felicitas were martyred. The Basilica, or town hall, was where trials were held. The 'basilica' shape, with an apse at one end (in this case the left) and columns along the sides, was to be adopted by the Christians for their churches. The Basilica at Leptis was actually turned into a church in the 6th century.

Early Egyptian Christianity

Adjacent regions often possess diametrically opposed viewpoints. While Tunisia and Numidia (the area of the Roman provinces of Africa and Mauretania) possessed a Christianity violently opposed to any accommodation to current culture, Egypt was to become the home of a Christian tradition that was ready to enter into dialogue with non-Christian philosophy. While the Christian philosophers of Alexandria were not fully typical of Egyptian Christians, they left their mark in an un-mistakable way not only in Egypt, but also in the Christian world at large.

The origins of Christianity in Egypt are very obscure. Until the end of the second century there is almost total silence. Later legend credited John Mark, the Gospel-writer, with founding the congregation at Alexandria. The mid-second century saw various heretics of Egyptian origin. It is only towards the end of that century that we actually know the names of orthodox Christian leaders from Egypt. The discoveries of papyri give a little more light. As we have seen earlier, the first fragment of the New Testament comes from Egypt (the Rylands fragment of John, dating from the first decades of the second century). This is only to be expected, since only the dry Egyptian climate allows perishable written material to survive. Fragments of various other books of the New Testament survive from the miscellaneous papyrus rubbish of second-century Egypt,[7] and large portions of papyrus books date from around AD 200.[8] There is also a very early account of the life of Jesus based on all four Gospels, a tiny fragment of Irenaeus's *Against the Heresies*, and some bits of a commentary, all coming from a similar period. From the next century there is quite a considerable amount of biblical texts, not to mention apocryphal works and Gnostic documents. Soon after this come the first fragments of Christian works in the Coptic dialects.

The silence of ancient writers has led many to believe that Egyptian 'Christianity' was at first almost completely Gnostic. This is almost certainly an overstatement. Gnostics from Egypt were prominent at an early date, but usually outside Egypt. Gnostics did survive for a long while in Egypt, but not necessarily because they originated there. The actual finds of papyri would suggest that Gnosticism followed on the heels of more orthodox Christianity. The survival of small Gnostic enclaves can be attributed to the intellectual bias of some Egyptian Christians. Another fact that enabled Gnostic sects to survive was the fact that their works were often translated into the

[7]Details in B. M. Metzger, *The Text of the New Testament* (OUP, 1964).
[8]*E.g.* Chester Beatty Papyrus of Paul's letters; Bodmer Gospel of John; another Bodmer Papyrus containing Luke and John.

Coptic dialects. They could then survive among the stolid Coptic-speaking peasants, even after the Greek-speaking congregations had been purged of heresy.

There was always a rift between the Greek-speaking élite and the Coptic-speaking substratum of peasantry in Egypt. This was eventually to divide the churches of Egypt, when in the fourth and fifth centuries doctrinal debates came to the fore. The bishops of Alexandria drew much of their support against the official theology of the Byzantine patriarchs from among the slow but intransigent Copts. Along with certain

A manuscript in Coptic, the language of Egypt, containing the end of Deuteronomy and the beginning of Jonah. It is in the Sahidic dialect. Early 4th century AD. British Museum, London.

other churches, Coptic Christianity supported the Monophysite movement, which held that Christ's humanity was
totally absorbed by His divinity.[9] They supported it to the
extent of murdering patriarchs who disagreed with them, and
would even appear at councils of the church to enforce their
views by violence.[1] But this story belongs to the fifth century.
When Christianity first emerges into the light at Alexandria,
its form is that of an educated and sophisticated group of
Greek-speaking intellectuals.

The teachers of Alexandria

Later historians, such as Eusebius, talk of a Catechetical
School of Alexandria (a School of Instruction for Christians).
Such a high-sounding title probably gives respectability to a
more informal group where earnest inquirers could learn of
the Christian philosophy, with baptism as a natural sequel to
intellectual conversion. The first leader of this group was
Pantaenus. He was a Sicilian by birth, but we know little else
about him for certain. Whether he became a Christian in
Sicily or Egypt is not known, but he was highly travelled
(Eusebius says that he went as far as India). In the second half
of the second century, we might have found him doing work
similar to that of Justin Martyr at Rome, providing a quiet
meeting-room, where people could come and discuss and
study, and where each Lord's day the little congregation met
to celebrate the Christian mysteries.

Clement of Alexandria

Pantaenus was followed in his work by Clement of Alexandria.
He was born in Athens of pagan parents, but seems to have
become a Christian in Alexandria. Did he join Pantaenus's
study-group while coming from Athens to complete his
education? After his conversion, he became an elder in the
local congregation, and was given the special task of teaching
those who were preparing for baptism. Clement was a com-

[9] See Glossary.
[1] Most general church histories give adequate coverage of the troubles in fifth-
century Alexandria due to the Monophysite dispute.

petent scholar, with more than a few of a scholar's idiosyncrasies. He had somewhat off-beat ideas, and a tendency towards mysticism and Gnosticism. He knew his pagan literature and religion well—so much so that he is one of our main sources for information about the mystery religions. But Clement was no compromiser. He describes something of the secret rites of those religions then current to expose them for what they are. He castigates their immorality and triviality. Then, having shown up their weaknesses, he commends the Christian philosophy as far more sublime and noble. But Clement was no cloistered academic. He has plenty of practical advice to offer on how a Christian should behave in the perverted world of second-century Alexandria. And in spite of his intellectualism, he emphasizes that it is at baptism that we become babes in Christ, and begin the travel towards true knowledge.

Clement was a commentator on the Bible, and bits of his studies in the smaller New Testament letters survive.[2] He also left a large amount of notes only partly arranged at his death. Clement was aware of the lure of Gnosticism but, although sharing something of its outlook, combatted its actual forms. In particular he attacks Gnosticism for its weak morality. To his mind, the Christian was the only person with the right to be called 'Gnostic' (the Knowing One), because only the orthodox Christian had access to the true knowledge of God.

Much else that Clement wrote has perished, but his surviving five works give us a picture of a very able advocate of Christianity, for circles where an intellectual approach was needed. But there was always the danger, in Clement's type of Christian, of making Christianity into a philosophical system. To Clement, true knowledge is all-important; the Lord's Supper (speaking of Christ's death) and the simple faith that will accept what God has done, do not always receive their rightful place. Clement left a wide-open door for speculation, and his successor Origen was to let his imagination run wild in remoulding Christian doctrine to his philosophical heart's desire. For, to Origen, knowledge of God through Christ the Revealer was almost more important than salvation from sin.

[2] Fragments from commentaries on 1 Peter, Jude, and 1 and 2 John.

At this point, however, the intellectuals of Alexandria went out on a limb. The parts of Clement's works in which he outlines Christian conduct are most akin to mainstream Christianity in Alexandria. This was the point where Christians could score and score again over their pagan rivals.

Persecution and expansion around AD 200

The third century began with persecution on a widespread scale. North Africa (where Perpetua and Felicitas and their friends suffered) and Egypt were among the places where churches were badly hit. Clement seems to have suspended his teaching activities and fled to Cappadocia, in eastern Asia Minor, where he ended his days.

The years after AD 200 found the Christian churches having settled the problems of Montanism, the date of Easter and the initial challenge of Gnosticism. Their next series of problems was not to be settled so easily; and all the while there was the ever-present threat of official hostility. Yet, in spite of this, Christianity was spreading. Even the imperfect picture that we possess is impressive. Not only were there Christian congregations well entrenched in Asia Minor; they were strong in mainland Greece and had made great strides in Egypt and North Africa. They had entered France and were firmly based in Rome. Further east they were spreading rapidly, some reports suggesting that they were established as far away as India. In the far west, Tertullian reports rumours of believers in Britain. This was also probably the time when the first congregations were formed in Spain.

How did Christians spread? The answer is that we know surprisingly little about the means used. Small meetings like that of Justin Martyr at Rome must have attracted outsiders and, as we have seen, we have evidence of similar activities in Alexandria. Later romances (such as the so-called *Clementine Recognitions*[3]) picture the apostles as preaching publicly, but this is unlikely to have happened while Christianity was still officially a proscribed cult. Even the speeches in Acts are mainly formal defences in court, or preaching in the syna-

[3] Romances about the apostolic period written in the fourth century, telling a far-fetched tale of the family of Clement of Rome.

gogue (which would have been no longer possible much after AD 70). Personal approach and argument were responsible for Justin's conversion, and Celsus bears eloquent testimony to how effective ordinary Christians were at this form of witness. The effect of Christian literature (such as the 'Apologies') is difficult to estimate. Equally, the martyrdoms must have influenced some people to inquire what made Christians stand firm under such pressure, but we have little idea of how many were so influenced. Some Christian groups, such as those at Vienne and Lyons, seem to have been largely expatriate groups

Mosaic from Hinton St Mary, Dorset, of the 4th century AD. One of the main figures, shown here, is seen with a chi-rho monogram (the first two letters of Christ's name in Greek, used as a symbol by Christians). The head is probably that of Christ, in which case it is the only known representation of Christ in a mosaic pavement anywhere in the Empire. British Museum, London.

in a foreign land. But, conversely, the martyrs of Scilli seem to have been a mixed bunch, with both Latin and Punic names.

The occupations of the converts may give some clue. Many were former philosophers, attracted by the combination of purity of life and a viable faith (polytheism as a philosophy was a non-starter). Some, notably from North Africa, were lawyers. One can possibly suggest that the orderliness of the Christian life attracted them. And here we may well touch the point where Christians made most impact. The Christian life lived out consistently against a background of sordid materialism spoke volumes. The effect of this was to attract inquirers to the little gatherings of Christians. But we know little of how individuals were contacted, and in the instruction of Christians much more emphasis was placed on personal living than on techniques of witnessing.

While Christians were spreading geographically, their extent in the class-scale was limited, although there were some in high places who were sympathizers, if not converts. A mistress of the repulsive emperor Commodus (an unworthy son of the philosopher-emperor Marcus Aurelius) was able to intercede successfully for Christians condemned to penal servitude in the mines of Sardinia.[4] Christians could be found in intellectual circles, and were sufficiently competent to be attacked by other scholars (a sure sign of being noticed and accepted). Christians in the army were scarce, mainly because enlistment involved acknowledgment of the state gods. There were some, however (perhaps converted after enlisting), and the Apologists attributed the episode of the 'Thundering Legion' (when a Roman army was saved from defeat by a sudden hailstorm which routed the enemy) to the prayers of Christians serving in the detachments involved. But the strength of Christians was at ground level. As small groups, with conspicuously Christ-like lives, they seized every opportunity to commend their Saviour, and the pagans among whom they lived took notice, and were often ready to inquire further.

[4]See below, p. 118.

7

Grounds for argument

The most violent quarrels are religious ones; and when strong characters are involved, and important theological points are being debated, the savagery of conflict is almost without parallel. Such troubles have always plagued the churches, and this period was well provided with internal wranglings which split congregations down the middle. At Rome there had been a number of quarrels during the latter part of the second century. But these pale into insignificance with the great wrangle at the beginning of the third century, when the church at Rome was divided over more than one issue. The protagonists in this struggle were Hippolytus and Callistus.

Hippolytus and Callistus

The sheer size of the capital city (perhaps a million inhabitants) ensured that the Roman church would be large, well organized and quite wealthy. The earliest underground cemeteries (popularly known as the Catacombs) owned by the Christian congregation probably date from this period, and they were sufficiently important to have special officials to look after them. The various congregations, each with their own officers, were watched over by the bishop, who had various assistants of his own. With a fair-size minority of members of non-Roman origin, it would have been strange if there had been no great differences of belief and practice. Three things combined to produce the ferment.

The doctrine of the Trinity was providing a fruitful subject for discussion and argument, and would do so for some while

Wall-painting from the Catacomb of Domitilla, Rome (possibly 2nd century AD), showing the Adoration of the Magi. The Catacombs were underground tombs; the Catacomb of Callistus was the burial-place of the bishops of Rome; their tombs can still be seen.

to come. Tertullian was addressing himself to the problem in North Africa just at this time. Secondly, with expanding congregations, there was a natural tendency to consider relaxing some of the very rigorous rules concerning personal conduct (for example a man who had been married twice could not normally become a church official). Lastly, the post of bishop of Rome was not unattractive. It was a position of considerable influence. When it became vacant, it was worth fighting for. This last reason almost certainly injected the venom into the clash between Hippolytus and Callistus.

The erudite Hippolytus is our source for the story. Naturally his account is biased; he has no good word for Callistus and very few for any who showed Callistus any sympathy. But Callistus was no white-washed saint. He had started his career as slave of a well-to-do Christian, but had got into trouble on charges of embezzlement. After a foolish attempt to escape from Italy, he was arrested and condemned to the treadmill by his master. But the Christians pleaded with Carpophorus, Callistus's master, and secured his release. The money was still outstanding, however. Callistus decided that as he had no hope of repaying, he would die a martyr. So he interrupted a service at a local Jewish synagogue, and was dragged before the city magistrate. He might have been executed as a Christian, if his master Carpophorus had not intervened; the sentence was deportation to the mines of Sardinia (the Roman equivalent of Siberia). His career might have ended there, but for one of the stranger episodes of church history. The Roman Christians had a friend at court, a concubine of the emperor Commodus called Marcia. As there were a number of Christians serving sentences in the Sardinian mines, the church leaders asked her to beg the emperor for an amnesty for them. Marcia succeeded, and an imperial official was sent with a list of the men to be released. Callistus's name was not on the list, but Callistus succeeded in getting round the official, and his

Glass perfume flask from the Catacombs, Rome, probably placed on a tomb. The anniversary of the deaths of the Christian martyrs was celebrated, and was to develop into a cult of martyrs. 3rd–4th century AD. British Museum, London.

name was added. On his return to Rome, Callistus found it politic to live quietly in a suburb, but he was soon to come back into prominence.

Hippolytus's own life-history is very obscure, but he was certainly a very erudite man with a strong tendency to despise the less-educated members of the church. He was well known as a biblical scholar and theologian, and produced a considerable number of works. He was also ambitious, and was probably aggrieved that after the death of Victor, the bishop of Rome, he did not gain greater prominence. Victor's successor, Zephyrinus, was none too well educated, but what really infuriated Hippolytus about him was that he took a kindly interest in Callistus! Callistus was ordained by Zephyrinus, in circumstances which Hippolytus does not describe. Then, much to Hippolytus's fury, Callistus swiftly became the bishop's right-hand man.

Disputes on the Trinity, and on forgiveness

Around this time there was considerable debate in Rome over the doctrine of the Trinity. A man from Smyrna, called Noetus, arrived in the capital and began propounding his own views. It soon became known that he had been expelled from the church at Smyrna for these very views which he was now propagating. The basic problem for anyone formulating the doctrine of the Trinity is to keep the balance between the belief in one God and the distinctive nature of the three Persons. Noetus proposed to evade the problem, by stating that God the Father took flesh and suffered and died for us as Christ (hence the name Patripassian for this heresy). Naturally such a solution makes Christ's conversing with His Father mere shadow-boxing, and is in conflict with the New Testament data. Followers of Noetus, notably Sabellius the Libyan, tried to deal with this criticism by suggesting that Father, Son and Spirit were 'modes' of God's appearing. But the church, standing firm on its traditional 'rule of faith', was not impressed. While the Eastern theologians would never countenance such ideas, there were many in the West who found them congenial. Hippolytus's own suggestion, that the differences of the Persons in the Godhead were based on difference of

119

function, is not too far removed from it. But one taunt of Noetus and Sabellius really stung. When they charged the traditionalists with worshipping two Gods, it roused them to fury.

Callistus could not help getting embroiled in the dispute. Whether from a desire to maintain peace, or because he supported Patripassian ideas, he managed to induce Zephyrinus to tolerate such notions. Hippolytus and his friends were furious. But since they were also trying to combat a more serious heresy in Adoptionism, they could not afford to be too fussy.[1] With the struggle dying down, Zephyrinus had died. Who was to be the new bishop?

Callistus was an opportunist in such matters, and made a swift move to gain popularity with the conservative section by denouncing Sabellius as a heretic—a cynical repudiation of a former colleague, according to Hippolytus. Whether this move gained him the necessary majority or not, he was elected bishop. Hippolytus's annoyance knew no bounds. Either immediately, or shortly after, he broke with Callistus and founded his own congregation. From there he sniped at Callistus, and the Roman church remained split for a generation.

Callistus gained more hatred from the stricter Christians by allowing even grave offences to be forgiven after penance. Hitherto it had been generally reckoned that sins such as immorality, homicide and apostasy were too grave to admit of forgiveness. An individual who committed such a sin could only be left to God's mercy, and was expelled from the Christian community. This problem of discipline was to cause many clashes in various churches. Tertullian, in North Africa, attacked a bishop for issuing an edict similar to Callistus's declaration of policy; some even think that Tertullian is attacking Callistus himself.

While Callistus and his friends were undoubtedly right in making some relaxation, Hippolytus and his friends were right in bewailing the drop in standards. Although even under Callistus's régime the penances were harsh, his act in opening

[1] Adoptionism was similar to Docetism, in stating that Jesus was merely a man, and that the divine Spirit came down upon Him at His baptism and left Him when He died on the cross.

the possibility of forgiveness of great sins would lead eventually to toleration of flagrant immorality on payment of a small indemnity. The trouble was that both were right. The church was called to be a congregation of saints. But saints are only sinners saved by God's grace. The forgiveness of Christ should not be denied to the penitent sinner. The difficulty was to know how this might be worked out in practice. Public declaration of forgiveness after penances involving several years' exclusion from communion was the way chosen by the early churches. But some smaller sects held more severe standards. Some sins were still held to be unforgivable, notably apostasy. This was to be the occasion of several savage disputes where personal differences were the real cause.

Hippolytus maintained his opposition even after Callistus had died. He also wrote prodigiously, even if there is some doubt over the authenticity of some works ascribed to him.[2] (Some scholars would, perhaps rightly, distinguish several Hippolytuses, who were later confused. By the time of Eusebius and Jerome in the fourth century most of Hippolytus's personal history was forgotten, though some of his works survived. Among these is his work against heresies, the latter chapters of which deal with Callistus.) For thirteen years Hippolytus continued his separate congregation, until in AD 235 both he and Pontian (the other bishop at Rome) were arrested in the persecution started by the emperor Maximinus Thrax. They were deported to Sardinia, and both died in the mines. When the persecution was over, both their bodies were brought back to Rome for burial, and the two communities managed to agree on a common successor. It would have been nice to think that the Roman church was to have some peace after this. However, only twenty years were to pass before the Roman Christians were again taking sides.

[2] The *Apostolic Tradition* is often said to be his, but has undergone much subsequent emendation. The real title of the work is now known to be *Ordinances of the Apostles*. When first discovered, it was known as the *Egyptian Church Order*, but R. H. Connolly proposed the title and the ascription to Hippolytus. This has been challenged by J. M. Hanssens and J.-P. Magne. The work survives only in various translations and emended versions, and there is often considerable doubt as to what was in the original. Its earliest parts are probably third/fourth century.

Origen: the early years

The early third century saw the persecution in which Perpetua and Felicitas were martyred at Carthage. This same persecution struck savagely in Alexandria also, and Clement had to flee the city. Among those who actually suffered martyrdom was a certain Leonides. His teenage son would have joined his father in the ranks of the martyrs, but for his mother, who hid his clothes at the crucial moment, no doubt not wanting to be deprived of her son as well as her husband. So the teenage would-be martyr was spared to become the greatest theologian of the persecuted church. His name was Origen.

Thanks to Eusebius, who was an enthusiastic admirer of Origen, we have a full account of his life.[3] Origen was born of Christian parents. Eusebius tells how he was for ever asking his parents hard questions concerning the faith, and how often his father would stand over the sleeping child wondering what would be his future.

After his father's execution, Origen's mother was left to look after a large family, and so Origen himself went to live with an aunt. This lady was a devotee of a Gnostic teacher called Paul, who held meetings in her house. But the heretic soon found that he had a sharp teenage critic in his audience, and it was probably not long before Origen moved elsewhere.

Origen had grown up in a Christian atmosphere from his earliest days, and the bishop of Alexandria, Demetrius, noticed his brilliance early. While Origen was still a teenager he took charge of Clement's old class, and gathered a group of earnest inquirers around him. One of these, Dionysius, was subsequently to take over Origen's work.[4] Another, Heraclas, eventually succeeded Demetrius as bishop. It was a mixed group, and some of the women who came were as outstanding as the men. For quite a number, however, martyrdom was the final event in their discipleship. Some, indeed, were never even baptized, but made their first confession of faith in blood. Christians at that time often talked of martyrdom as the 'second baptism'.

Being a Christian teacher, however, was not a paid post. It is unlikely that any church officials were paid at this time.

[3] The story is told in Eusebius *Church History* vi.
[4] For Dionysius's later career, see below, pp. 132, 135, 138 f., 142 ff.

Origen had to live somehow. He had studied under the best philosophers, including Ammonius Saccas, who was reckoned to be a Christian. Origen made a name for himself as a competent scholar, although his great rival, the pagan Porphyry, made sneering references to Origen's profession of Christianity. So Origen set up as a teacher. But it was a poorly-paid job, and he had to sell his library in order to eat. But the enforced austerity that he had to practise enhanced his reputation, and gradually the hard times passed.

Origen managed to travel widely, both to Rome and to Arabia. He visited Palestine and Syria, where he was invited to speak to local churches. Back in Alexandria, bishop Demetrius was annoyed because other churches allowed Origen to preach even though he was not ordained. But in reply to his complaints, the church leaders of Syria wrote back to say that it was not unknown for lay people to preach in their churches, and that the practice was not irregular. Origen returned to Alexandria, but gave up instructing candidates for baptism in order to devote his time to advanced study. His reputation as a philosopher was such that while in Palestine he had been summoned to the imperial court to meet the empress mother Julia Mammaea, the mother of the African emperor Septimius Severus. On returning to Alexandria, he found a generous patron. A wealthy man called Ambrose had been entangled with the Valentinian Gnostics. Origen had led him to a true faith in Christ, and Ambrose showed his gratitude in a most practical way. He provided Origen with shorthand experts and copyists to take down and reproduce copies of his writings, and from then on Origen became a subsidized scholar. Around 230, Origen again went to Palestine, where he was ordained 'elder'. This sparked off a further row, because according to conventions in the churches no eunuch might be ordained. Origen, in a fit of youthful stupidity, had mutilated himself, thinking that this was in accordance with Gospel precept. Demetrius, the bishop of Alexandria, was almost certainly moved by spite and jealousy, but his influence made Alexandria an uncomfortable place for the eccentric scholar. So, complete with Ambrose and the copyists, Origen moved to Palestine, where he was to spend a further twenty years in furious activity.

Julia Mammaea, mother of the North African emperor Septimius Severus: a bronze medallion from the British Museum, London.

Origen's writings and teachings

Origen's writings cover a vast range. He was the first textual critic of the Bible. His mammoth six-fold edition of the Old Testament (the *Hexapla*) would have made his reputation if he had done nothing else. In this he set out in successive columns the Hebrew text, the Hebrew transliterated into Greek, and the four Greek versions (*i.e.* the Septuagint, Aquila, Symmachus and Theodotion). In places, additional versions brought in as many as nine columns (*e.g.* in the Psalms). One of the sources for the Psalms was a scroll which he found in a jar near Jericho—almost certainly the first of the Dead Sea Scrolls to come to light! Origen went to the trouble to learn Hebrew (although he never became very good at it), and was the first person to try to make a scientifically reliable text of the Old Testament.

He wrote commentaries on nearly every book of the Bible, and at one time nearly 500 of his sermons survived. Like many of his contemporaries, Origen favoured the allegorical method of expounding the Scriptures. The reason for this was a desire to make every verse of the Bible speak in a relevant manner to his contemporary situation. So when genealogies or Old Testament history or parts of the law-codes seemed to have little to say on a literal plane, he would delve deeper in order to find a more satisfying message. In fact, Origen was so eager to look for the 'inner meaning' of a passage, that often he would pass over the literal meaning entirely. This was a dangerous practice, especially when the expositor was a man like Origen, with a fertile mind and a philosophical system waiting to be read into any convenient Scripture passage.

Yet despite this, when it came to apologetics, Origen was a sharp controversialist. He dealt out a crushing reply to Celsus' attack on Christianity, pointing out in particular the excellency of the Christian life. He showed up much of Celsus' criticism to be uninformed and shallow (Celsus did not know the difference between Gnostics and orthodox Christians), and he effectively silenced the attack on Christianity from the intellectual side. One more fascinating discovery of recent years is a verbatim account of a theological debate which Origen held with some Arabian bishops. This work, the *Conversation with Heraclides*, was discovered on a papyrus found in a quarry at Toura near Cairo in 1941.[5] The work records a discussion on a multitude of theological topics, especially the deity of Christ and the resurrection and the nature of the soul in man. Such a record is almost without parallel, and sheds a fascinating light on a group of theologians thrashing out a problem with an expert.

Origen's largest work is a systematic theology, called *Concerning the Beginnings*. Unfortunately, this work has survived mainly in an emended version. In the later years of the fourth century, Origen became theologically suspect, and friends of his re-issued his works with alterations to make them more acceptable. At times the changes seem to have been quite large, for we do possess considerable fragments of the Greek original, as well as the Latin expurgated version.[6]

Origen's ideas were to have a vast influence on Eastern theologians; any short summary of them will be grossly inadequate. His idea of the Trinity as a graded hierarchy was to lie behind the controversy between Athanasius and Arius and their followers in the next century. In sharp contrast to the

[5] Further details in F. L. Cross, *The Early Christian Fathers* (Duckworth, 1960). pp. 132–133.
[6] The Latin version was issued by Rufinus of Aquileia, at the end of the fourth century, when many churchmen, led by Jerome, were denouncing Origen as a heretic. The issue was partly a matter of church politics, but certain way-out ideas of Origen were formally condemned (*e.g.* the suggestion that eventually the devil might repent and be saved) insofar as they departed from apostolic doctrine.

Western way of thinking, which began from God's unity and then discussed the three Persons, Origen began with the three. His notion of God the Father as the sole source of all deity could be pressed to the extent of making Christ a second and inferior god. Origen drew a clear distinction between Christ and His Father, so much so that he was even ready to use the term 'two Gods' if it was properly safeguarded. Like many Eastern theologians, Origen has very little to say on the doctrine of the Holy Spirit. Although the deficiencies of Origen's Trinitarian theology were rectified in the definitions of the next century, another of his ideas had a very long life. This was his doctrine of the atonement. Origen had no doubt about the power and reality of the devil, and he considered that mankind was justly in the devil's grip because of sin. But, in attacking Christ, the devil overstepped the just claims that he had against sinners, and in consequence he was deprived even of his rightful prey by way of punishment. This idea of Christ's death as a ransom paid to the devil, and the cross as a means of deceiving and defeating him, was to remain the most common way of viewing the work of Christ until the time of Anselm, in the eleventh century. But although many theologians were prepared to follow Origen at this point, few would stay with him when he wandered on to explore the possibilities of the eventual total destruction of all evil. Origen pioneered the hope that in the end perhaps all would be saved, and even Satan would cease to be evil, and finally God would be all in all. In Origen's hands this idea did not preclude the necessity of God's judgment on the wicked, but it was a rash speculation for which he was later censured. At times Origen could wander off into what was almost a vague theosophy, but he usually tried to cover himself by saying that these speculations were meant only for the élite, and that simple Christians should concern themselves with the simple gospel and the practicalities of Christian living.

Later ages were to count Origen as the father of both orthodoxy and heresy. Certainly, some of his passing thoughts could be abused, and in some of his speculations he went far off the beaten track of the biblical data. But in his defence it should be said that he always was ready to resist the vagaries of Gnosticism and the attacks of pagan philosophy. When we realize that all this was done between periods of persecution, it stands as a worthy achievement.

But Origen was not allowed to end his days in peaceful study and speculation. When the Empire-wide persecution under the emperor Decius broke out,[7] Origen could not escape notice. The emperor decided that the defection of such an outstanding advocate of Christianity was something much to be desired. Origen was tortured relentlessly, but refused to yield. When the persecution ceased with the death of Decius, Origen was released. He lived on for a few more years, but died in 253. His death was certainly hastened by the treatment he had received. Perhaps it was just as well that some of his more weird ideas were not given a halo of sanctity by the martyrdom of their author. Instead, Origen stands second after Tertullian in the ranks of those whom later ages called neither heretic nor saint.

[7] See below, pp. 130 ff.

8

Collision course

The Roman Empire AD 200–250

The second century AD, which forms the backcloth to the crucial period of the expansion of Christianity, was a time when the Roman Empire reached and passed its zenith. It was a time when peace was normal, and when strong and efficient emperors ruled with a generally benevolent despotism. The following century was to see the Empire almost collapse under the onslaught of outside enemies, only to take on a new lease of life for a further century and a half.

Without a doubt, some of the weakness was caused by internal factors. When the emperor Caracalla extended Roman citizenship to all free men in the Empire in AD 212, it was not done with any benevolent motive in mind. The Empire needed more taxes. Citizens paid taxes. Therefore make more citizens. Also, to echo the immortal words of that arch-cynic Tacitus, the secret was out that emperors could be made elsewhere than at Rome. The benevolent Antonines (Trajan, Hadrian, Antoninus Pius) had chosen their successors according to merit, until Marcus Aurelius (who followed Antoninus Pius) let his son Commodus succeed him. Commodus was murdered on the last day of 192, after a reign in which he had flaunted his vices and shown himself to be an unworthy son of a moral if eccentric father. On his death there was a general scramble for power, from which the energetic North African Septimius Severus emerged triumphant. The unstable Severan dynasty, which he founded, wallowed on in the blood of its various members, finally ending with the murder of Alexander Severus in 235.

The Severi had managed to hold things in check, and at

Septimius Severus and his wife, Julia Domna: a relief from the Arch of Septimius Severus, Rome. The emperor and his wife are shown sacrificing with their heads covered, as was customary.

times had been mildly favourable to the Christians, but the year 235 saw the rise to power of the bestial giant Maximinus Thrax (a peasant from Thrace, in northern Greece, who rose to power through the army; he is said to have been eight feet tall and of massive physique). Under Maximinus Thrax persecution broke out. But by now the menace from outside the Empire was almost overwhelming the frontiers. The Persians had destroyed the moribund Parthian Empire beyond the Euphrates, and were making considerable inroads into Roman holdings in Syria. The Rhine-Danube frontier was under continual threat along its whole length from northern barbarians. Then, in 238, internal strife broke out again. Maximinus put down four rivals before he was at last killed. Gordian III succeeded in stabilizing the Eastern frontier before he was murdered. His successor, Philip the Arabian, was certainly a sympathizer with the Christians, but in 249 he was defeated by Decius at Verona.

The persecution under Decius

The new emperor was to have only a short reign (249–251), but the Christians were to have good reason to remember it. Decius was a Roman of the old school, and decided that all the new-fangled decadence would have to go. His coinage illustrates the point, for he issued commemorative coins for all the respectable Roman emperors. Among the things which he considered to be the causes of the decline of the Roman Empire was the rising Christian movement. He decided that it must be eliminated. A general edict was issued requiring every-

The emperor Decius: portrait on a coin. British Museum, London.

body to sacrifice to the gods of Rome, and to obtain a certificate of the fact! Nothing like this had ever been done before. From the surviving certificates in Egypt,[1] we know that even avowed pagans had to satisfy the authorities. One pagan priestess records indignantly that she had sacrificed to the gods all her life. But the edict came as a hammer-blow to the Christians, and its effects were almost disastrous.

A change had come over the churches in the early part of the third century, taking place so gradually that probably no-one noticed. The church was beginning to become respectable. People like Origen had done much to make Christian belief intellectually acceptable. Christians had consistently lived down the old slanders of cannibalism and immorality in their meetings. Better-class people were taking an interest in the churches, and even the imperial household had not been implacably hostile. The little congregations were becoming larger. Their officials were more numerous, and growing in importance. The church at Rome furnishes a good example, because we know that even after the persecution of Decius its officials were as follows: one bishop, forty-six elders, seven deacons, seven subdeacons, nearly a hundred minor functionaries such as readers and door-keepers. The church supported over 1,500 needy persons.[2] This was surely the realm of big business.

Along with the growth in numbers had come, inevitably, a lowering of standards. The cost of being a Christian was not quite as high as it had been. Martyrdom was still a possibility, but a fairly remote one. You might be insulted for being a Christian, or be ostracized by your friends, but there was un-limited friendship to be found in the Christian community by way of compensation. In fact, there was now good reason for joining the church for other reasons than allegiance to Jesus Christ. It was not the last time that church leaders were to be-moan the poor quality of the contemporary Christian gener-ation in contrast to its predecessors. And it was at this point that the imperial edict came.

Inevitably, such an edict hit the socially prominent first of

[1]Example given in J. Stevenson, *A New Eusebius*, pp. 228–229.
[2]Numbers given by Cornelius, bishop of Rome, to Fabius, bishop of Antioch. J. Stevenson, *A New Eusebius*, pp. 264–265.

all. Church leaders were among the first to be challenged. Some, like Fabian of Rome, or Babylas of Antioch, or Alexander of Jerusalem, paid for their loyalty to Christ with their lives. Not all leaders were so brave or so loyal. Some went into hiding. Cyprian of Carthage was one of these, and he was to suffer severe censure for so doing. Dionysius of Alexandria might have joined the ranks of martyrs, but on the news of his arrest one of his congregation raised a private army who rescued him under cover of night while he was being taken under guard to Alexandria for trial. Dionysius spent the rest of the persecution evading the authorities.

Other Christians who fled were less fortunate. Some from Egypt and Syria died while they fled into the arid deserts, or, like one old bishop and his wife, just disappeared. Others were captured by wild natives and enslaved. But it was depressing how many Christians neither stood firm nor attempted to escape. Many were informed against by pagan associates, and were dragged before the authorities to be made to sacrifice to the gods of Rome. But many came willingly, even on occasion led by their own bishops! But for every one who actually sacrificed, there were probably several who obtained the necessary certificate without having to go through with the act itself. Certificates could be bought or forged, and in a crowd passing an altar it would not be too hard just to slip by without taking part. So various people adopted various expedients.

The problem of lapsed Christians

But Decius soon died, killed fighting against the Goths on the Danube frontier. His successors had neither inclination nor time to continue his policy, even if it had a logical continuation. The churches were left with the task of sorting out the mess. Their task was not helped by one old custom. It had long been normal for those under sentence as Christians to be held in high esteem by the churches. Their very words were treasured. There is even some evidence that they were consulted over the truth or otherwise of the prophecies of Montanus at the end of the second century. But their greatest privilege was the power to forgive those who had failed to stand firm under persecution. Originally such a right would have been exercised perhaps only in prison.[3] Once arrested, Christians had been liable to death whether they recanted or not. But in the aftermath of Decius's persecution a new situation had arisen. Many had fallen, or at least had gravely compromised their position. Many churches were at that moment leaderless. The 'confessors' (those who had actually suffered in the name of Christ) were in a position to absolve, and many were eager to have such absolution. Some unscrupulous people even issued certificates of forgiveness in the name of deceased martyrs. In one such instance the fraud was quickly spotted because the martyr who was supposed to have issued the certificates had been illiterate![4] This was the position which confronted many new bishops, as well as those who had come out of hiding to resume their work. And nowhere was the situation more difficult than for bishop Cyprian at Carthage.

Cyprian and the lapsed Christians

Like Tertullian, his great fellow-countryman of the previous generation, Cyprian was a lawyer by profession and became a Christian only in middle life. But he was a learned and energetic convert. When the position of bishop of Carthage fell vacant, many were willing to vote for him. And so, in spite of the fact that he had been a Christian only for a few years, he found himself bishop of the leading church of North Africa. Opposition still remained, and Cyprian was not universally liked. He was a man with a strong sense of dignity, and was not amenable to being contradicted. His own opinions and the will of God sometimes became inextricably confused in his mind. But in spite of his faults, he was an eminently suitable bishop to lead the North African churches. Before any trouble could break out internally, Decius's persecution had begun. Cyprian decided that it was politic to be out of town and to look after the churches from a country hide-out. So he lay low until the storm was past. On his return he found an exceedingly awkward situation.

[3] An example of this occurs in the account of the martyrs at Vienne and Lyons in 177.
[4] Cyprian reports this. See J. Stevenson, *A New Eusebius*, pp. 232–233.

There was a considerable clamour from some sections for a general amnesty. But Cyprian, true to the tradition of North African Christianity, was reluctant to grant it. There were others who were clamouring that the claims of the 'confessors' should be recognized. But Cyprian silenced them, for the moment, by saying that martyrdom was the glory of the church in general, and that the bishop as leader of the church was the proper person to decide how to dispense the benefits that the martyrs had gained. This meant that Cyprian was to be the final arbiter. There was a third group, however, who were to give him most trouble. These were the old hard-liners, who refused to consider any relaxation of the rules. They held that those who had compromised themselves under persecution must remain excluded. Ultimately, they were to split off as a separate group.

Cyprian, as a good lawyer, tried to have everything cut and dried. To have actually sacrificed to the pagan gods was a terrible sin, and for such he proposed that they could not be received back into membership except when dying. Cyprian was too humane to cut them off entirely. When it came to the larger number, who had merely obtained a certificate without actually sacrificing, he was ready to allow them back after suitable penance. This might seem fairly lenient, until we remember that penances might involve several years' exclusion from communion. Naturally, Cyprian could not please everyone. There were howls of protest on all sides, but eventually only the hard-liners remained irreconcilable. They gathered all the malcontents together, but found their greatest support overseas.

Novatian: schism again at Rome

The church at Rome had been split only a generation before over who should be the bishop. Now there were two candidates again, Cornelius and Novatian. Cornelius seems to have been a man of unexceptional ability, but one who commanded more general support. Novatian was brilliant. He was a competent theologian, and a work on the doctrine of the Trinity survives to give an idea of his prowess. Even his enemies had to admit that he was blameless in his life, and had been a zealous worker up to the time of the election. But like Hippolytus before him, he was an extremist. No doubt this was because he still held to the idea of the church as a pure society, an embattled minority in a hostile world. This would have been laudable if it had stopped short of harshness towards the weaker brethren. Maybe it was this trait in his character that lost him the election. Anyway, there were soon two bishops of Rome contending for recognition.

Cyprian was confronted with letters from both factions at Rome. Both asked for acknowledgment. Cyprian found himself in an advantageous position, because certain dissidents from Carthage had tried to enlist help from Rome against him at an earlier date. The Roman elders had even written Cyprian a censorious letter, presumably making nasty suggestions about Cyprian's prudent flight from Carthage during the persecution. At the time, Cyprian had had to content himself with scathing remarks about the bad grammar of the letter and the poor quality of the paper on which it was written. Now he found himself in the position of arbiter. Cyprian allowed himself the privilege of making quite sure that Cornelius had been properly elected before acknowledging him as legitimate bishop. He even wrote a tract on the unity of the church to elaborate his views on the subject.

Novatian's appeal to Cyprian came shortly after, but did not receive a warm welcome. He had also written to bishops of various Eastern churches, and might have fared better there. Dionysius of Alexandria, now out of hiding, was not inclined to be harsh with him, and suggested that he could easily clarify his own position by accepting Cornelius's election, and that there would be no blame attached. But tempers in Rome had become too heated, and Novatian set up his own congregation. He even, in Cyprian's eyes, had the effrontery to appoint a 'true' bishop at Carthage! But the reverberations were to continue. Marcian, the bishop of Arles, came out in support of Novatian, and was therefore deposed. But the little sect of Novatianists continued to survive until well into the next century. When Constantine came across them, he is reputed to have told one of their leaders, 'Well, you will be the only one climbing up your ladder to heaven.' They survived as an exceedingly strict sect, until an imperial inquiry found that they were not heretical enough to be excluded from the universal church. Even when tolerated, Novatianist churches lingered on, occasionally suffering some harassment from officious leaders of the state church.

Cyprian's teaching

Next to Tertullian, Cyprian is the earliest Christian Latin writer of whose work a considerable amount survives. He was an indefatigable letter-writer, and also turned out various tracts on many topics. He has been credited with many changes in Christian doctrine, but such a suggestion would have surprised Cyprian himself, because he aimed to be conservative and to keep to precedent wherever possible. For example, Cyprian certainly drops various hints which if taken together could be seen as the foundations of the doctrine of the mediaeval mass. But in his most extended treatment of the subject,[5] when he is combatting a move to use water instead of wine at the communion, his main concern is that everything should be done just as the Lord did. He takes over the widely-held assumptions about the eucharist being the 'Christian sacrifice', without questioning whether they were in fact a valid exposition of the Old Testament sacrificial code as it was to be observed under the new covenant. This was precisely a lawyer's fault. The Old Testament had prescribed sacrifices. The Old Testament was the law of God. Therefore Christians must have a sacrifice. This sacrifice was also Christ's sacrifice, which was in some way tied in with the eucharist. This was Cyprian's line of reasoning, and he felt that he was being perfectly traditional and biblical.

The same thing could be said of Cyprian's doctrine of the church and ministry. For him the Christian bishop was equivalent to the Old Testament high priest.[6] The church was the Christian version of the nation of Israel, with clear boundaries beyond which there was no salvation. Each church had only one legal bishop, who could trace back his legal succession to the apostles, of whom Peter was the leader. This seemed perfectly clear and simple to Cyprian. Anyone who

[5] Cyprian, *Letter* 63.
[6] He normally calls the bishop *sacerdos* (Latin for priest).

differed from him must be knowingly perverse.

However, Cyprian was legislating for his own situation, and his own opinions could be modified. In view of what was soon to happen, he cannot be invoked as a supporter of a mediaeval Romanism which he never knew.

Cornelius died without enjoying his hard-won office for long, and after one successor who lived for an even shorter period, the Roman church gained another leader of a very different stamp. When Stephen became the bishop of Rome, Cyprian found him at first an ally in dealing with Marcian, the bishop of Arles who had thrown his lot in with Novatian. But soon they were to clash. The repercussions of the persecution of Decius were still being felt. Far off in Spain, two bishops had led their flocks in public apostasy.[7] The loyal members of their congregations had deposed them and appointed successors. But the two deposed officials had gone to Rome and had gained Stephen's support. When he wrote back to their churches demanding that they should be reinstated, the churches replied by appealing to Cyprian. Cyprian promptly wrote to Stephen, giving him a verbal rap over the knuckles for such an action. The outcome seems to have been that Stephen climbed down, but he could not have liked Cyprian for what he did. Soon he was to have opportunity for revenge.

The controversy over 'rebaptism'

The continued success of the churches meant that many people from very peculiar backgrounds were becoming members of Christian congregations. The various odd sects of Gnostics were becoming weaker, and many were leaving their weird fantasies for the more straightforward faith of the mainstream churches. Soon questions were asked about what was to be done with these people. Most churches were content to receive them formally with the bishop laying his hands on them in blessing. But some asked whether they had in fact been baptized. The answer was probably 'Yes', but doubt remained. In North Africa, however, the situation was quite plain to church members. Since heretics could not be part of

[7]Leaders of the churches at León and Mérida. For the whole incident see J. Stevenson, *A New Eusebius*, pp. 248–250.

the church, and since entry to the church was by baptism, any-one coming from outside must be baptized. This was really the more logical position, as long as Christianity generally held together. It did not have in view the existence of separate groupings of churches with relatively orthodox beliefs. Equally, it allowed tolerance between churches, so long as they agreed on the essentials of Christian belief. But when Stephen heard of the peculiar practice of the churches of North Africa, he immediately saw a chance to attack Cyprian. But he chose the wrong man to attack.[8]

Stephen opened his attack by writing to Cyprian and his colleagues, calling on them to desist from their improper practice. Cyprian's reply was to call a council of North African bishops in Carthage to uphold their practice. They rallied round and affirmed that their practice of rebaptizing heretics had been done from time immemorial (i.e. from at least the start of the century). Stephen, like his predecessor Victor, decided to take a tough line. He tried to excommunicate Cyprian. It was a foolish move. Cyprian could count on support from many quarters, even those where local churches did not agree with his particular practice. A scathing letter came from Firmilian, the bishop of Caesarea in Cappadocia, supporting Cyprian and censuring Stephen most violently. Dionysius of Alexandria intervened, telling Stephen that he must retract. All of North Africa shouted defiance at Stephen and ridiculed his claim to act as judge. From all sides came the resolute enunciation of the right of each bishop to form his own judgment under the sole direction of Christ. We do not know whether Stephen backed down in person, or whether death intervened and his successor had no desire to perpetuate the quarrel. Certainly Stephen was dead before many months, and Cyprian lived to enjoy his triumph. Sixty years later, in the calm of better days, the churches finally arrived at a compromise. Baptism was to be accepted if it had been proper Trinitarian baptism; otherwise the person concerned was to be rebaptized.

The eventual decision on baptism is in some ways typical of the general trend of thought. The danger of a quasi-magical

[8] The best account of the dispute is in J. Stevenson, *A New Eusebius*, pp. 251–258.

idea of the sacraments had been creeping in since Tertullian's time. It is significant that Cyprian was an enthusiastic advocate of infant baptism.[9] His reasoning, that baptism washed away all guilt, and that even babies had inherited guilt that needed removal, does not appeal to many today. But the worst feature was that it treated baptism as a magical act. Infant baptism was a long way from becoming normal; only babies who were likely to die were baptized. Adults remained the main candidates for baptism with a period of instruction culminating in baptism early on Easter morning, with communion for the first time immediately afterwards. Cyprian had been a true traditionalist in insisting that baptism was the entry into the church. His definition of the church may have been slightly narrow in excluding the theologically blameless Novatianists. But the tide was against him, in separating baptism from the church, and so moving away from the apostolic practice.

Persecution under Valerian

While the Christians were picking up the pieces after Decius's persecution and fighting various feuds, the Roman Empire tottered on the verge of collapse. There were several claimants for the throne, and there was only a measure of stability when Valerian siezed power in 253. Valerian took a neutral attitude to the Christians for a while, but then resumed persecution, according to Eusebius at the instigation of a certain court astrologer.

The attack was directed mainly against leaders of the Christian community, but was not pressed home very severely. Dionysius of Alexandria again found himself in court, but was only deported to a remote oasis. There his missionary efforts forced the authorities to bring him back nearer the city where they could keep a more effective eye on him. Once more, as during the Decian persecution, the worst damage was done by the Alexandria mob. They ran riot and tore to pieces any Christians they could find. The governor gave them plenty of encouragement, and the churches went underground. Else-

[9] Cyprian, *Letter* 61 deals with the practice. It is perhaps noteworthy that Cyprian denies that baptism is in any way equivalent to circumcision under the old covenant.

where, there were some martyrs. At Rome the bishop and four deacons were arrested after a service at a cemetery, and were executed. At Carthage, Cyprian was arrested. He was summoned to appear before a court, and on his refusal to renounce his faith he was exiled to a suburb of Carthage. With the advent of a new governor, Cyprian was called back to court. After the briefest of hearings, Cyprian was condemned to death for being a Christian. A large crowd gathered outside one of the gates of Carthage, and witnessed the execution. Cyprian faced death with grave dignity. As a Roman citizen, he was beheaded. The crowd watched with almost religious reverence. The church of the martyrs of North Africa now had a martyr-bishop.[1]

Valerian's persecution faded out gradually. Within two years of Cyprian's death Valerian himself had been captured by the Persians, and spent the remainder of his life in captivity. His co-emperor Gallienus (his successor) set about beating back the barbarians. Where he was ineffective, local military commanders took the initiative, and even set themselves up as emperors. These local emperors are sometimes called the Thirty Tyrants, but they effectively stemmed the invasions. However, Gallienus's accession also brought peace for the Christians. They were officially allowed to meet for worship, and to own buildings and cemeteries.[2] In its typically offhand way, the Roman state gave official recognition of the existence of a group who were fast becoming a force to be reckoned with in the Empire.

It is perhaps significant that this period sees the last of the Apologists. Minucius Felix is otherwise unknown, but his little Latin dialogue between a Christian and a pagan is instructive, if only because it is the first work of its kind which ends in the conversion of the non-Christian. The dialogue is set in an atmosphere of calm, the arguments are slight and predictable, and the outcome seems to occasion nothing but naïve joy. Christianity was moving perceptibly into a place where it will

[1] The account of Cyprian's martyrdom is in J. Stevenson, *A New Eusebius*, pp. 260–263.
[2] Edict in J. Stevenson, *A New Eusebius*, pp. 267–268.

be at least tolerated. The move was not to be entirely without incident, however.

9

Towards stability

The latter years of the third century saw the Christian churches enjoying a period of relative calm and considerable prosperity. With the toleration edict of Gallienus, the situation was now reasonably secure. Christians could meet for worship without fear, and their organizations were afforded some recognition. Also, a new generation was arising, and the spirit of the martyrs and clandestine meetings had given way to an era of churchmen and respectable ordered gatherings. Some men survived from the earlier epoch, but they were soon sub-merged in the new age.

One such survivor was Dionysius, the highly durable pope of Alexandria (the title 'pope' could mean any high church dignitary; Cyprian was commonly called the 'pope' of Carthage; the word is a familiar term of address, meaning 'father'). Dionysius could look back to his training under Origen, in the early days of the century. He had taken over from Origen the task of instructing candidates for baptism, and was no mean theologian. Eusebius preserves for us an interesting piece of his work, an attempt to show that John's Gospel and letters were not composed by the same man who wrote Revelation. Like his earlier namesake at Corinth, Dionysius was a prolific letter-writer, and again Eusebius preserves fragments of his work. Almost alone among the bishops of the prominent churches, Dionysius survived both the Decian and the Valerian persecutions, and survived them with credit. His subsequent career mainly concerns two con-troversies, one concerning Paul of Samosata, the other with his namesake Dionysius of Rome.

The emperor Gallienus, who issued an edict allowing Christians to worship and to own buildings. A coin in the British Museum, London.

The affair of Paul of Samosata

The career of Paul of Samosata shows how high an able man could rise, even when known to be a Christian. Our knowledge of this extraordinary man comes exclusively from his enemies,[1] but even they had to give him credit for his ability. Following the emperor Valerian's disastrous capture by the Persians, the Roman Empire's eastern frontier was maintained only with the help of the state of Palmyra, ruled by the highly capable Queen Zenobia. Her chancellor, and the bishop of Antioch as well, was Paul of Samosata. We know very little about Paul's earlier history, but he seems rather out of place against the severe background of Syrian Christianity. One could well ask how far his behaviour was consistent with a Christian profession, but in fairness one must say that we know of him only through the reports of implacable opponents. He lived in a style which befitted the chancellor of Queen Zenobia, and in such a position he was unassailable. But his theology was considered suspect, at least by the men from Origen's school. It is reported that he held 'low and degrading views about Christ'. The meaning of this is far from clear. Some think that he held a form of Adoptionism,[2] while others believe that he was reacting to the tendency of making Jesus so heavenly as to be inhuman.[3] But when all was said and done,

[1] Mainly in the account of Eusebius, *Church History* vii. 27–30.

[2] See Glossary (also under Docetism).

[3] There were later on two streams of thought regarding the Person of Christ. The Alexandrine school tended to stress the divinity of Christ to the exclusion of His humanity, and could lead to Monophysitism (see Glossary). The Antiochene school, which some think began with Paul of Samosata, could overstress the two natures in Christ to the extent of making Him a split personality.

143

it was Paul's display and popularity that really annoyed the other bishops. Paul of Samosata was the first 'prince bishop', and he held court in state. The services he conducted were noted for their elaborate ceremonial. He also had the temerity to get rid of old hymns and have new ones composed. Furthermore, although not even his enemies could prove anything, he was certainly very popular with the ladies of his congregation. Finally, the bishops of the neighbouring churches managed to get Paul to debate his views with an elder from Antioch called Malchion. Only a few tantalizing fragments of this disputation survive, but both sides seem to have given good account of themselves.

Further synods of bishops were held. Dionysius of Alexandria, who had been watching events carefully, was invited to attend, but had to decline through ill-health. Cyprian's old ally, Firmilian of Caesarea, attended the first two councils, and died while travelling to the final one. The necessity to hold councils over and over again must be indication that either Paul of Samosata was not without support or it was exceedingly difficult to convict him of any specific error. But at the last council Paul was condemned. A circular letter, much of which survives in Eusebius's account, was sent from the council to the various churches, telling everyone of Paul's deposition. There was only one problem. He would not go! For four years the defiant bishop held out, until in 272 Queen Zenobia was defeated by the emperor Aurelian, and Paul of Samosata was deprived of the queen's protection. The enraged bishops appealed to the emperor to remove Paul from the church building so that his successor could move in. Since the original letter from the council had been sent to the bishop of Rome, and perhaps because he was the leader of the church in the capital city, Aurelian decreed that he and the bishops of Italy should appoint a successor. They supported the decisions of the council, and the Roman soldiers saw to it that Paul of Samosata departed. We know nothing of his subsequent career, although groups of his followers are reported in the next century, and his name was anathematized in the various decrees of councils for a long time afterwards. But this was the first time that the state had intervened in a church dispute. It was not a happy precedent.

Dionysius of Alexandria and Dionysius of Rome

Before the affair of Paul of Samosata, Dionysius of Alexandria had been involved in another dispute. Following the persecution of Valerian, the Roman church had appointed another Dionysius to be their bishop. Dionysius of Alexandria, in the course of his duties, had stumbled on what he thought was heresy in the region of Cyrene. He found some people holding beliefs like those of Sabellius the Libyan, namely a view of the Trinity which blurred the distinction between the Persons. Dionysius of Alexandria, as befitted a theologian, set about refuting the error. But he let himself go too far. Some of his statements went to the other extreme. His formulation of a doctrine of the Trinity almost amounted to a loose association of three Gods. Western theologians, and the Roman church in particular, could be expected to be furious at such ideas. Someone told Dionysius of Rome what his namesake of Alexandria had said, and there was trouble.

Dionysius of Rome wrote a very stiff letter. His fellow-bishop in Alexandria was left in no doubt that some people were very worried about his orthodoxy. Fortunately, Dionysius of Alexandria was a very good explainer. He pointed out that the suspect phrases should be read in context, while admitting that he might have overstated his case in order to make his point. This took the steam out of the dispute, and it seems to have closed amicably. Its main interest is that it foreshadowed the disputes of the next century, when both sides in the Trinitarian controversy[4] were to claim that they were faithful followers of Dionysius of Alexandria.[5]

Dionysius may have been very glad to get out of this spot of trouble with relative ease, because he had other problems on his mind. He had to deal with hotheads who looked forward to the reign of Christ on earth as a sensuous paradise (perhaps this explains why he took a rather jaundiced view of Revelation). He also had to look after his church during a terrible plague. Here again, the Christians distinguished themselves by selfless behaviour, tending the sick and burying the dead

[4] See Glossary (also under Arius and Athanasius).
[5] Our main information about this dispute between the two Dionysii comes from Athanasius' references to it. See J. Stevenson, *A New Eusebius*, pp. 268–271.

145

while the pagan inhabitants fled like panic-stricken animals. There were plenty of cases where sick pagans were abandoned by their own families in the streets, only to be picked up and nursed by Christians. Quite a number of Christians who could have escaped the plague by leaving the city stayed behind on purpose to look after the sick and dying, and eventually died of the disease themselves. Remember, too, that some of those sick and dying pagans who were cared for had probably been members of the Alexandria mob which ten years before had been on the rampage lynching any Christians that they could find.

It is probably during this period that the earliest version of the Scriptures were made in Sahidic, the Coptic dialect of Upper Egypt. Soon the other dialects, Bohairic (spoken around the Nile delta), Fayumic and others had their own translations. Soon the Coptic Christians outnumbered the Greek-speaking Christians. They were to prove a thorn in the flesh for many later patriarchs, being somewhat akin to the North Africans in zeal, and having a certain intransigence of their very own.

Further expansion

While Dionysius was fighting his various battles, the expansion of Christian churches continued. In north-eastern Asia Minor Gregory the Wonderworker carried out considerable evangelistic activity, and that whole area was to become a stronghold of Christians. Gregory came from an eminent family (his brother-in-law was a provincial governor), and had studied under Origen in Caesarea, where both he and his brother-in-law had been converted. He spent the rest of his time evangelizing and teaching, in spite of various interruptions due to barbarian invasions. This was the time when the Roman Empire was narrowly avoiding total collapse, yet the Christians seem to have found civil disruption little hindrance. Gregory's influence was great. He was among those present at the synod which condemned Paul of Samosata, and his pupils included Macrina, the grandmother of Basil the Great and Gregory of Nyssa, the foremost theologians and church statesmen of the late fourth century.

About the church further east our information is scanty. The Syriac-speaking Christians were extending their influence beyond the imperial frontiers. One piece of evidence comes from the excavations at Dura-Europos, a town on the Euphrates, on the eastern frontier of Syria. Here a small Christian church was discovered. As the town was destroyed in 256, the church building must date from before this time. It was here that a tiny Greek fragment of Tatian's *Diatessaron* was discovered, and the building itself is notable for the decorated plaster on its walls. But it is reasonable to suppose that this would be only one church among many. Christians were making headway to the north in Armenia, and this country was to be the first to adopt Christianity as its official religion early in the next century.

In the western Mediterranean area, there is good reason to think that Christian churches were still mainly found in towns (in fact the very word 'pagan' means countryman). As we have seen, in Spain there were sizeable churches in several towns,

The Roman amphitheatre, Arles. A church council was held at Arles in 314.

and in France the area of Provence and the Rhône Valley was probably well provided with little Christian communities. There were certainly a few congregations of Christians in Britain by this time. We hear of three British martyrs by name in the last great persecutions, and three bishops from Britain attended a council at Arles in 314 shortly after the persecution was over. Meanwhile, in the areas where Christianity had been long established, the congregations there had undergone considerable change. What would they have been like now? How far did they differ from Justin's little meeting in the upper-storey room in Rome around the middle of the previous century?[6]

Christian worship in the third century

The first difference that we would notice would be the great increase in numbers. The congregation would now be no mere handful, but a large gathering. Also, there would be many more officials. Probably by this time, too, the church would be meeting in a building erected specially for the purpose.[7] The building would probably resemble the local town hall or 'basilica', though it would be less pretentious. It would be rectangular in plan, with a semi-circular apse at one end. In this apse there would be a chair for the local bishop, with seats for the elders arranged on each side. In front of these seats would be the altar-table, very much in the shape of a table, made either of wood or stone.[8] This end of the building might be on a slightly raised platform. The rest of the building would be empty, without seats and, apart from perhaps some painted design on the wall-plaster, it would be unadorned.

The door-keepers admitted the worshippers, and often men and women were segregated on opposite sides of the church. The service would divide into two parts, the preaching and Bible reading coming first, followed by the eucharist. Assistant clergy would read the lessons and conduct the prayers.

[6] See above, pp. 70 ff.

[7] The first record of a church building specifically used for worship comes from the record of a building in Edessa destroyed by a flood in about AD 250.

[8] The stone variety would often have a wooden top. The tomb-like stone altar seems to have come into fashion after the time of Constantine when church-buildings were often erected around a martyr's tomb.

The 'basilica' form, adopted for early churches from the Roman town hall plan. (1) **Mosaic showing a 'basilica' church,** with an apsidal end on the right. From a 6th-century mosaic in the Basilica of St Euphrasius, Poreč (Yugoslavia). (2) **The Roman Basilica, Trier.** Originally the audience hall of Constantine's palace (built c. 300), this basilica has been restored and is now a church. Trier was established as capital of the Western Empire under Constantine's father Constantius.

149

The prayers would still be extempore, but their form and content would be fairly predictable. We have samples of prayers from this period on papyrus from Egypt, which bear every sign of having been written down for a particular occasion. Only the closing doxology is in a fairly stereotyped form, and the prayers were sufficiently ephemeral for people to write out their shopping lists or a bill on the back of the papyrus afterwards. Congregational hymn-singing was unknown as yet,[9] but there might be solo singing, if a suitably gifted man was a member of the congregation.

The climax of the first part of the service would be the sermon by the bishop. After this, all those unbaptized would be sent out, after receiving the blessing of the bishop. The doors would be shut, and the faithful would greet each other with the kiss of fellowship. Then the bread and wine would be brought, and the rite of the eucharist would take place. The congregation would take part only in a few responses, which would be known by heart (the dialogue beginning 'Lift up your hearts', still used in the Anglican communion service, was certainly in use at this period[1]). The bishop's great prayer of thanksgiving would still probably be extempore, but its theme of God's acts in making and saving mankind would recur Sunday after Sunday. The congregation might well join in the hymn of the seraphs, the 'Holy, holy, holy' of Isaiah 6. Then one of the lesser clergy would call the people to receive the elements of the communion. They would file up in front of the altar-table to receive the bread and wine. The service ended with a short prayer and the dismissal, 'Depart in peace'. In Latin-speaking churches, the dismissal ('Missa' in Latin) eventually became the term by which the whole service was known, and so gave birth to the English word 'mass'. In the Greek-speaking East the churches kept to the older term 'eucharist' (meaning 'thanksgiving'), a rather more appropriate description.

The great festivals of the churches were Easter and the festivals of the martyrs. Christmas was generally celebrated

[9] It was first popularized by Ambrose of Milan in the last decades of the fourth century.
[1] Cyprian mentions it as already in use in his time. It also occurs in the so-called *Apostolic Tradition*.

in the West only after the triumph of Constantine, when the time of Christ's birth was reckoned to coincide with the day of the Unconquered Sun on 25 December. It was not until the last years of the fourth century that Christmas became a regular festival in the Eastern churches. Many of them continued to celebrate the birth of Christ on 6 January, as they had done before.[2] The only other annual festival in most churches was Pentecost (or Whitsun), celebrated by both East and West fifty days after Easter and marking the end of the Easter festivities. In this period between Easter and Whitsun it was considered improper to kneel when praying, this being considered to be a sign of mourning.

Easter was the normal time for baptisms. Some weeks before Easter, names were taken of those who desired to be baptized. The candidates were carefully scrutinized, to see if their general behaviour made them fit to be received. Some occupations were considered as incompatible with Christian discipleship. Not only gladiators and actors had to give up their jobs before being accepted as candidates for baptism: the schoolmaster (because he taught the tales of classical mythology) and the painter and sculptor (because their work could be used in the service of idolatry) also had to find other employment. After scrutiny, the candidates underwent special instruction from the bishop, with the assistance of the other clergy.[3] Of prime importance was the learning of the creed, which had to be memorized and recited. After fasting and having various exorcisms pronounced over them, the candidates came to the evening before Easter day. After a vigil lasting most of the night, they were brought to the place of baptism at first light on Easter day. Originally this would have been in some convenient river; by this time, however, many church buildings had their own baptistry. The candidates were asked in turn to renounce Satan and to declare their allegiance to Christ. Then they were baptized three times, replying 'I believe' to three questions which were the basis of the creed which they had learned. (It is virtually certain that creeds as we know them, such as the Apostles' or the Nicene

[2] Certain churches which today keep this date are not perpetuating old usage.
[3] From the fourth century we possess several complete series of lectures given to candidates for baptism.

Wall-painting from Lullingstone Roman villa, Kent (*c.* 350), from a Christian chapel in the villa. From the original plaster found (see left of photograph), the remainder of the painting has been restored to show six figures praying. Another wall has a painting of a chi-rho monogram. The chapel at Dura-Europos in Syria was similarly part of a larger villa.

Creed, were originally in the form of questions put to candidates at baptism.) After baptism, the candidates were brought to where the rest of the church congregation was assembled. Often the newly-baptized were dressed in special white robes. The eucharist or communion service followed immediately, and Easter day was begun as a day of rejoicing.

Church organization

Allowing for local variants, what we have just described would be the main worship in the churches, on average Sundays. Obviously, when there were baptisms, or on the anniversary of a martyr, or when some church officials were being appointed and ordained, the actual form of service would vary.[4] But it should be stressed that at this period there was nothing like a fixed verbal form (as in the Anglican Book of Common Prayer or the Roman Catholic Missal) for the services. The

[4] Our information comes from two works, manuals on church order; the *Apostolic Tradition* (see above, p. 121 n. 2), and the *Didascalia* (a work written in Syria). Both probably date from the late third century.

nearest approach would be a traditional order of doing things, and this would be subject to considerable local variants.

Ordinations usually took place before the communion service. The local bishop ordained the lesser clergy, who would anyway be acting as his assistants. The local congregation elected its bishop when the post became vacant, and he had to be formally ordained by at least three bishops of blameless character and orthodox beliefs. But since each town and village would have its own bishop presiding over the congregation, this would not present too many difficulties. Some bishops of larger towns tended to exert a primacy over their particular area (*e.g.* the bishop of Alexandria in Egypt; the bishop of Carthage in North Africa). They would preside when councils were called, and in time this system formalized to give rise to the great patriarchates of later church history. But when a council was called, every bishop had the right to stand up and speak, and matters of concern were settled by voting of all present, not by the chairman's authoritative pronouncement.

The individual church had considerable duties besides Sunday worship. The deacons were responsible for a large amount of poor-relief, and would carry this out under the supervision of the bishop. Then there would be formal instruction of candidates for baptism, and weeknight meetings often held in homes. Some bishops might teach, or even en-

153

gage in commercial activities, but this was frowned upon. Others were rich enough to own and farm estates, while (as we have seen with Paul of Samosata) one could even combine the offices of bishop and magistrate.[5] Then there would be the burial ground that needed supervision, not to mention correspondence on various matters and the travelling of officials to regional meetings. From this period some of the day-to-day paper-work of the churches survives. The papyri of Egypt[6] have examples of prayers, both public and private, hymns (one complete with tune!) and lists and letters in abundance. The church was a business; but unfortunately the cares of the world were often likely to crush the spiritual life. This tendency should not be exaggerated, however. The records of the last great persecution were to show that the churches were much better able to withstand persecution than they had been in the time of Decius.

Theology of the average church member

What did the average church member understand of his faith? He would certainly not be well versed in the speculations of Origen, nor would he be likely to be an enthusiastic would-be martyr. First and foremost, the Christian of this period would be certain that he worshipped the true God, as opposed to the many idols of the surrounding paganism. He was also thoroughly convinced that God was almighty, and was the Creator of the physical world. Then he would know of God's saving acts in Christ, although the actual connection between God the Father and Jesus would not be worked out in any thoroughness. Salvation was seen as the reward for faithfulness to God and Christ—faithfulness worked out in regular attendance at worship and in a life lived under the direction of God's law. Baptism was operative in starting this life, and communion was necessary to provide power to continue. For the future there was the glorious hope of heaven for the faith-

[5] This became much commoner after the time of Constantine, when the local bishop was often the best educated and most reliable man available!

[6] The most famous collection is the Oxyrhynchus Papyri, collected by Grenfell and Hunt in 1899–1900. Twenty-four volumes at present have been published. See also G. A. Deissmann's *Light from the Ancient East* (Hodder and Stoughton, 1927).

ful and the terrifying prospect of hell for unbelievers. This would sum up the beliefs of the average Christian. He would listen with interest as theologians tackled the minutiae, but theological battles would be of little interest to him.

It was only in the peace of the era after Constantine that theological points were debated in the market-place. Before this, a fairly united front was presented to the paganism outside. But in a superstitious world, it was only to be expected that superstition would exist among Christians. The average church member would not be surprised to hear of miracles attributed to apostles and other holy men and women. He would view the martyrs with veneration, and would be perfectly prepared to believe that they were interested in the churches that they left behind. He would see baptism and the eucharist as great mysteries, to be approached with reverence —the reverence due to the God who alone could defeat the demonic powers who were manifestly at work in the surrounding paganism. The Scriptures themselves were treated as God's oracles, the true oracles as opposed to those demonic counterfeits from Delphi and elsewhere. The Scriptures were seen not only as straightforward writings, but also as works with secondary meanings, where the real truth was hidden and had to be extracted by means of careful investigation. To hand over the Scriptures to hostile pagans was treated as the next worst crime to apostasy itself. Such reverence also brought about the reticence about writing down or divulging the text of the creed, the special secret which each Christian memorized before his baptism. Above all, there was the consciousness of God which pervaded the lives of Christians and provided the motivation for lives that were signally different from those of their pagan neighbours.

10

The last battle

The last decades of the third century are lacking in great events and great men among the churches. Eusebius was born in these years, and remembered many of the church leaders. He loads them with praise for being good pastors and often learned men, but there is no denying that they did not seem as outstanding as the men of the previous generation. But when Eusebius also says that in his considered opinion the final great persecution came on the churches as a judgment for their worldliness, the praise which he has previously handed out looks rather tarnished. But if the last decades of the third century were uneventful and without great spiritual movement for the churches, in the outside world some very important developments were taking place.

Two movements on the intellectual front of the world at large require consideration. The first of these is the growing syncretism in religion and a growing weariness with paganism. The many sets of gods were becoming intermixed, and the regional differences were getting blurred. Easy communications helped this. Soldiers recruited in Britain might well serve on the Euphrates frontier. Merchants travelled far beyond the Roman frontiers, reaching both China and Ireland.[1] Philosophies and deities were passed round and shared. There was a tendency for people to think that the various deities were really only different names for one great power. The philosophical climate of the day encouraged this, because Neo-platonism treated the variety of things on earth

[1] See Sir Mortimer Wheeler, *Rome beyond the Imperial Frontiers* (Penguin Books, 1955).

as the shadows of a few great universal concepts. So a variety of gods could all be different names for the same power. The Egyptian Isis, Artemis of the Ephesians and the Syrian Astarte could be equated. The Greek Zeus, the Roman Jupiter, the Egyptian Amon-Re and even the Jewish Yahweh could be invoked as the names of the one great Power. Various myths were looked on as alternative versions of the truth. This trend at times even went almost as far as a kind of mono-theism, as when Constantine's father Constantius directed all his worship to the 'Unconquered Sun', as the supreme high god.

Alongside this, the old cults were losing their enthusiastic devotees.[2] And for the first time Christianity was becoming a religion of the countryside, instead of the faith of small groups centred in towns. Rural areas of North Africa, Egypt, Syria and Asia Minor were being Christianized to an astonishing extent. Temples were falling into decay, and the crowds were now turning towards the Christian churches. This movement was to receive one jolting setback in the final great persecution, but after that it would run on as an invincible flood. Against this only the mystery religions and cults like that of Mithras still held a fascination. But it was only the lofty and noble aspects of the old religions which held the imagination of the earnest pagan. Cults were mostly treated as tools for magical purposes, or as excuses for revelry. When the average pagan left them in preference for the Christian church, it may well have been that he saw the advantages of being the supporter of a more powerful deity and nothing more. Certainly, in the years that followed, leading Christians would have to denounce the questionable celebrations that lasted all night long at various martyr tombs, and the superstition which would treat relics of saints, and even the communion elements themselves, as material for quasi-magical purposes.

One other movement needs at least a passing mention the Manichees. In some ways this was the last of the Gnostic heresies, and had much in common also with the syncretism of the period. But it was destined to become a world movement

[2] Some very impressive evidence in W. H. C. Frend, *The Early Church* (Hodder and Stoughton, 1965), pp. 121–123.

and to trouble the churches well into the Middle Ages.[3] The founder of the movement, Mani, was born in Persia, and began his preaching in the middle of the third century. He professed to amalgamate the message of Buddha, Zoroaster and Jesus, with himself as the final revelation. The rigid fatalistic determinism of Manicheism was to appeal to the young Augustine[4] towards the end of the next century. In the period now under discussion it was seen as a seditious threat because of its Persian origins. No account was taken of the fact that Mani had been brutally executed at the instigation of the Zoroastrian priests of Persia. Manicheism was officially pro-scribed by the emperor Galerius.[5] The Christians watched with approval as the imperial agents destroyed the sacred books of the Manichees; but soon it was to be the turn of the Christian Scriptures to be burned.

The Roman Empire: rescue and reform

The latter part of the third century saw the Roman Empire almost collapse, then eventually recover. Gallienus, who had proclaimed toleration for the Christians, ruled from 253 to 268. He was not in control of the Empire for the whole of this time, however. Various local rulers proclaimed themselves as emperors. The Roman Empire owed its survival to their ability, coupled with the inability of the barbarians to unite to deliver a crushing blow to the whole imperial structure. In the East, Macrianus forced the Persians back to the Euphrates. Postumus ruled in France, Spain and Britain, and not only kept the German tribes at bay but also withstood the various attempts of Gallienus to recover these provinces which Postumus ruled. AD 268 was a year of chaos in which both Gallienus and Postumus were murdered by their troops. The Alemanni and the Goths saw this as a chance to invade the Empire, but the new emperor, Claudius Gothicus, defeated them so heavily that they were not to be a danger again for many years. Claudius Gothicus died of the plague after only

[3] See G. S. M. Walker, *The Growing Storm* (Paternoster, 1961), pp. 149–151.
[4] See Glossary.
[5] Information collected in J. Stevenson, *A New Eusebius*, pp. 281–283. Manichean writings also survive among the Egyptian papyri.

two years' reign, but his successor Aurelian was another soldier-emperor. He not only put down the various local emperors, but also stabilized the whole of the Empire. He finally ended the little empire of Queen Zenobia at Palmyra (as we have seen, she had been the protectress of Paul of Samosata[6]), but before he could settle the issue with the Persians he was murdered by some of his own officers. An interregnum and the short reign of the emperor Tacitus (275–276) followed. This aged emperor (he was seventy-five when appointed) died from the rigours of a victorious campaign in Asia Minor, but his successor Probus was able to continue the work of reconstruction. Probus reigned six years —no mean feat in such troubled times—and was able to give attention not only to repelling barbarians but also to patching up the shaky economy of the Empire. Continual wars and invasions had played havoc with farming, the coinage had suffered several large devaluations since the end of the second century, and the small farmers were being forced to sell up and join the ranks of the unemployable poor of the cities. These economic ills were to be present as long as the Roman Empire lasted, in spite of many attempts to rectify them. Then, when Probus was killed by mutinous soldiers in 282, there was another rush to seize imperial power. From the ensuing three years' chaos, Diocletian emerged supreme, and immediately decided to reorganize the Empire.

Diocletian's plan was to have four emperors, two for each half of the Empire. He was the senior emperor of the eastern part, with Maximian as his colleague in the West. Under them were two junior emperors, Galerius in the East and Constantius (the father of Constantine the Great) in the West. It was agreed that after twenty years the two senior men would abdicate in favour of the two junior, and two more junior emperors would be appointed. Apart from a breakaway emperor in Britain, who was not suppressed until 296, the system worked well. But it did mean that East and West began to get out of step. Diocletian's reforms in fact marked the beginning of the division of the Empire into East and West. Such were the events through which Christians lived during the last years of the third century.

[6] Above, pp. 143 f.

The emperor Diocletian: a bust in the Museo Capitolino, Rome.

Diocletian was an able ruler, and in temperament exceedingly placid. As long as he could keep the Empire on an even keel, he was not too worried about the cults which might exist inside it. His junior colleague in the East, Galerius, was a more impetuous man, and highly superstitious. Diocletian could not have helped noticing that Christians were everywhere, and that they were powerful. When a usurper was besieged in Alexandria, it had been the local bishop who had acted as intermediary between the rebels and the government troops surrounding the city. Diocletian and Galerius had already officially proscribed the Manichees on the grounds that their cult was seditious. Galerius viewed the Christians with similar ill-will. One of our authorities for this period, Lactantius, was a Christian who was a tutor at the imperial court. He attributes Galerius's hatred of Christians to pressure which his mother exerted on him. All the ingredients for a witch-hunt were there in force. The superstitious Galerius, egged on by his mother, had secret meetings with Diocletian. Diocletian called advisers to further private sessions. Not content with that, they sent away to the oracle of Apollo at Miletus to get advice. Eusebius even suggests that Galerius bribed various oracles to give pronouncements unfavourable to Christians. In the end Galerius got his way, and the last great persecution began.[7]

The final persecution

Diocletian and Galerius had set up their court at Nicomedia, on the eastern shore of the Bosphorus. Close to the palace was the impressive building of the church at Nicomedia. The city was hardly awake when the imperial guardsmen broke into the building, and set about wrecking it. They could find no image of any god, but they burned any copies of the Scriptures that they could find. The whole place was torn apart and finally demolished. While people were still numb with the shock, an edict was posted. By the orders of the emperors all church buildings were to be demolished, all copies of the Scriptures were to be destroyed, and all Christians in public positions were to be deprived of their rank and reduced to the status of slaves.

A purge of Christians in the army may have begun before the publication of the edict. But now any prominent Christian was in danger. One such Christian official retaliated in an obvious if foolhardy way. He tore down the imperial edict. He was immediately seized and put to death. Mob violence seems to have run ahead of official policy, but soon the old edicts of Decius were revived.[8] Christians were to be compelled to sacrifice to the state gods, by torture if necessary. Meanwhile, the attack on property was carried out ruthlessly.

The minutes of the search of a church building at Cirta in

[7] Eusebius, *Church History* viii and ix is our primary source, supplemented by Lactantius's work, *On the Deaths of the Persecutors*.
[8] See above, pp. 130 ff.

North Africa survive.[9] The mayor of the town, accompanied by officials and soldiers, arrived at the church building. The clergy (consisting of the bishop, three elders, two deacons and various minor officials) were summoned. The church property was turned out, and an inventory made. The haul was not impressive. There were a few articles of silver plate, but the movable property was mainly clothes and shoes for distribution to those in need. The main object of the search was to find the Scriptures. The church officials were not very cooperative, but they used only passive resistance. Each tried to shift the responsibility on to someone else, especially if that person was not there. At this time the attack was against the books, not against the persons of the clergy. Various tricks were tried at Cirta and elsewhere to satisfy the officials conducting the search. Some tried to salve their consciences by handing over non-Christian writings or heretical works; after all, the public slaves would not be intelligent enough to tell the difference. Many ignorant soldiers seem to have gone off with a book that they thought was a Bible but was in fact some treatise on medicine or astrology! When the persecution was over, years later, the public records of searches and the details of those who had handed over books were often raked up to discredit those who had since then become prominent church leaders.[1] On the side of the Roman officials, there was concern to carry out the letter of the law, but no desire to be overthorough. And so, at Girta, they cleared out what movable property they could, collected such books as were easy to find, and departed. But soon the harassment that started in 303 was replaced by open persecution.

In a large and rambling empire, such as the Romans held, the carrying out of imperial edicts varied from one place to another. In the West, where Christians were not numerous, the persecution was perfunctory. Constantine's father contented himself with a few measures against church property, and refused to condemn Christians to death. In France and Spain there was little done in the matter of destroying the Scriptures. But in the eastern part of the Empire the persecu-

[9] Translated in J. Stevenson, *A New Eusebius*, pp. 287–289. This took place in AD 303.

[1] See J. Stevenson, *A New Eusebius*, pp. 308–310, 328–329, for post-persecution sessions of recrimination.

tion was harsh and unrelenting. Eusebius, who was to be court bishop under Constantine, was twice in prison for his faith, and saw his learned teacher Pamphilus (who had studied under Origen) executed for refusing to sacrifice. Eusebius saw at first hand the brutalities of the persecution in Egypt and Palestine, and has left us horrifyingly graphic accounts of them. Our other main informant, Lactantius, was a tutor at the imperial court. He had been trained in North Africa by Arnobius, a pagan rhetorician who had shocked everyone including the local bishop by deciding to join the Christian church towards the close of his life. To prove his sincerity, Arnobius wrote a long defence of his new-found faith, in which he delivered a violent attack on all images that were worshipped. Lactantius was more gifted than his teacher, Arnobius, and he used his abilities well. While still at court he wrote a detailed Apology for the Christian faith in seven books, to combat the derogatory remarks of a high official there. When the persecution broke out, Lactantius lost his post, but managed to fade away quietly. He took refuge with Constantine and after much hardship eventually regained his old post after Constantine's complete victory. As an old man, he wrote a semi-historical work, showing how all the persecutors of the Christians had come to violent or degrading deaths.

Persecution after Diocletian's abdication

The violence of the persecution was largely due to the fact that power was changing hands at the imperial court. Diocletian was a sick man, and Galerius had assumed effective control. In May 305, Diocletian abdicated, along with Maximian, his co-emperor in the West. Constantius became ruler of the West, and Galerius took over in the East. With Constantius in power, the persecution petered out in the West, but not before the forty-seven members of a little church near Carthage had suffered martyrdom en masse. Rumour had it that the bishop of Rome, Marcellinus, had offered sacrifice. It is probable that he did something which could be construed as betrayal, but we have no way of telling how bad it was. Certainly there were too many church leaders who either gave way or compromised their position.

For the Western churches, the ordeal was reasonably short, and the damage not too great. The persecution was to have one terrible legacy, however: it planted fresh seeds of strife in North Africa. The diehards, the confessors of the faith and all in sympathy with the ideals of Tertullian and Cyprian, were to form a coalition which was to set up a 'church of the martyrs' against the 'church of the traitors' (*i.e.* those who were thought to have handed over the Scriptures). The breakaway group were led at first by Donatus, who gave his name to the dispute. They were to prove an insoluble problem to Constantine and his successors, who tried alternate periods of conciliation and coercion with equal lack of success. The Donatists proved a terror to the more respectable 'Catholic' congregations of North Africa, and their more violent members used terrorism and nationalistic revolt to further their own ends. The eventual result was to weaken the North African churches to such an extent that they vanished without trace under the impact of the Muslim invasion. That final catastrophe, however, lies beyond the confines of our study.

In the East, Galerius had a ready helper in the person of Maximin, the new subordinate emperor. So the persecution was continued with great savagery. Edict after edict was issued demanding that all should sacrifice to the ancient gods. An attempt was made to revitalize paganism. High priests were appointed in imitation of the Christian bishops. The old slanders were raked up again, and Christians were accused of all kinds of revolting practices. Maximin even had forged 'Memoirs of Pilate' circulated and taught in schools in an

Galerius (left), emperor of the East, and Maximin, his co-emperor: coins from the British Museum.

attempt to discredit the beginnings of Christianity. But the Christians were equal to that game. They not only produced their own versions of the 'Memoirs of Pilate' (equally fictitious but highly laudatory of Jesus), but they even published works showing the errors in the pagan versions. Militant paganism could still have its devotees, as we can see from an inscription from Arycanda in southern Asia Minor which petitions that the 'atheists' should be destroyed.[2] But in general the devotees of paganism were those who saw this fad of the emperor as a means of personal advancement.

Eusebius describes how the weight of the persecution fell in Syria, Palestine and Egypt. Bishops and ordinary Christians suffered all kinds of death as the persecution-fever ran riot. Eusebius quotes a letter from an Egyptian bishop (Phileas of Thmuis, in the Nile delta). The letter was written from prison, and the bishop describes the deaths of many Christians who refused to sacrifice to the idols. He exhorts his readers to stand faithful. Soon after, he left them his own martyrdom as an example.

But persecution in Egypt was not the only trouble which afflicted the churches there. While Peter, the bishop of Alexandria, was in prison, another bishop called Melitius took it upon himself to organize the Egyptian Christians. This might have been forgiven if it had been a temporary measure, but it was not. Melitius intended to be successor to Peter, and was aiming to present the churches with a *fait accompli*. But his plan was not successful. He received a letter of censure from four clerics who were in prison awaiting execution—a most damaging thing because the word of the 'confessors' was exceedingly influential. He was disciplined after the persecution was over, but he had considerable support from among the Coptic-speaking peasants, and the split in the churches was not easily healed. It was the first sign of the troubles that were to divide Egyptian Christians later. When in the early fourth century the great champion of orthodox Christianity, Athanasius,[3] became bishop of Alexandria, one of the less creditable episodes of his career was the repression of the

[2] Translated in J. Stevenson, *A New Eusebius*, p. 297.
[3] See Glossary.

165

followers of Melitius with considerable brutality.[4] This led to Athanasius' first banishment by Constantine.

Elsewhere, in Asia Minor, the persecution was equally fierce. One small town, where all the inhabitants were nominally Christian, was besieged by government forces and razed to the ground. A Christian who was an imperial finance minister was executed for refusing to recant. But even while the persecution was at its height, the arch-persecutor was dying. Galerius had suffered from a very painful illness for a long time (probably cancer of the bowels), and he was dying in considerable pain. His hatred of the Christians had not abated, but his trusted helper Licinius extracted a repeal of the persecuting edict from the dying man. The new edict gave grudging acceptance for Christians, although censuring them for their folly in deserting their ancestors' gods. It was the work of an embittered but hopeless man. Within a week Galerius was dead.

Politics and moves towards toleration

With the death of Galerius the position was as follows. Galerius's junior colleague, Maximin, and Licinius ruled the East between them, while Constantine controlled most of the West except Italy, where a rival emperor, Maxentius, had control. This Maxentius was the son of Diocletian's colleague Maximian, who had abdicated with Diocletian in 305. But Maximian had not been willing to shed all his power, and he had later tried to regain control of the West. His son had been associated with him in this plan, but it had been only partially successful. The son, Maxentius, had gained control of Italy and North Africa, but Constantine had defeated and killed the father, Maximian, and so held the rest of the Western Empire. Constantine himself had not been an official nominee for imperial power, but on the death of his father Constantius at York in 306 he had taken over his position as emperor of the West. In the general chaos he had been accepted by the other men in power. He had been successful in repulsing barbarian

[4] Papyrus letters from the Melitian side are edited in H. I. Bell, *Jews and Christians in Egypt* (British Museum, 1924).

Constantine (left) and his rival, Maxentius, whom he defeated at the Battle of the Milvian Bridge in 312. Two gold medallions from the British Museum, London.

invasions from across the Rhine, and his position grew stronger.

In the East of the Empire, Licinius had extended his power as far as the Bosphorus against Maximin (still in theory his colleague), and was beginning to make overtures to the Christians in Maximin's dominions. Constantine in the West had a political interest in all this, for he was no friend of the house of Galerius who had tried to keep him in custody at Nicomedia to prevent him joining his father Constantius. So, mutual hostility to Maximin drew Constantine and Licinius together, and Maxentius, the Western rebel-emperor, started to ally himself with Maximin.

Maximin had never liked the grudging toleration of the Christians that had been wrung from the dying Galerius. He gave open encouragement for the renewal of persecution in the areas that he controlled. Among the last victims of the persecutions were Peter of Alexandria and Lucian of Antioch. Lucian is a shadowy figure, but although only a elder he had taught most of the men who were to hold important office in the churches under Constantine. His pupils were directed in the line of Origen's work, and some were to give support to Arius and his heresy. But there was no suspicion of Lucian's orthodoxy, and he died a martyr. Peter, the bishop of Alexandria, had been in prison for his faith before, and was the chief victim of the pogrom directed against the Christians of Egypt. While in prison he had tried to check the interference of Melitius, who was acting the part of bishop of Alexandria unofficially, even threatening in one letter to deal with Melitius personally when he got out. He never lived to fulfil this threat, however.

But Maximin had other problems besides the Christians. A campaign he led against the Armenians was a failure, and he feared that Licinius would strike against him. Since the Armenians had recently made Christianity the official religion of their country, Maximin's repulse was considered in Christian circles as an 'act of God'. Then a plague broke out as well, and the behaviour of the Christians during the plague earned them many sympathizers. Meanwhile, in the West, Constantine decided that the time was ripe to overthrow his rival Maxentius.

Maxentius still held Italy and North Africa, and was not unsympathetic towards the Christians—at any rate, he left them alone. But with Licinius holding Maximin in check, Constantine now had the opportunity to get rid of Maxentius, whom he viewed as an awkward interloper with no official status. Constantine crossed the Alps in the spring of 312, but it took him much hard fighting before he reached Rome in late October. While preparing for the next move outside the city Constantine had his famous vision.

Constantine's vision and victory

Our accounts of Constantine's vision come mainly from Eusebius and Lactantius. Both knew the royal court, but both were Christians. We know from pagan sources also that Constantine had some sort of vision which convinced him that God was on his side. This additional information makes it likely that Eusebius and Lactantius are recording actual events, and not engaging in convenient rationalization after the event. From Constantine's subsequent attitude towards the Christians, we may assume that he himself believed that the God of the Christians had met him and helped him.

Estimates of Constantine vary. To some he is the great hero, the first Christian emperor and the equal of the apostles. To others he is a double-dyed villain who did the devil's work most effectually. Certainly he was neither. To judge from his subsequent career Constantine was no cunning schemer. His behaviour as self-appointed chairman at church councils, and his obtuseness in dealing with church affairs show him to be a man with only moderate intelligence, but without any sinister intent. From his father he inherited a belief in a supreme God, which was something more than a mere idea that there was 'something' there. Above all, he was a practical man, and would be prepared to use anything that would work. The favour of the God of the Christians was something which he considered worth having, and he probably equated this God with the god which his father worshipped. Therefore, he set out to try and do the things which would please this God whose favour he wanted.

Constantine had fought his way as far as the city of Rome, and was encamped north of the city, in the suburbs beyond the river Tiber. Winter was nearly on him, and he was not equipped to face a long siege. Moreover, Maxentius had already shown himself to be well able to hold off formidable

The Milvian Bridge, Rome, scene of Constantine's vision and his victory over Maxentius. The bridge was originally built in 109 BC.

The Battle of the Milvian Bridge. A relief from the Arch of Constantine, Rome, depicting the battle.

attacks against the city when there had been an attempt to dislodge him some years before. So Constantine needed help, and needed it badly. Eusebius says that he saw a vision, and later received instructions in a dream. Lactantius mentions only the dream. Both agree that Constantine was instructed to put the sign of the Christian cross on his soldiers' equipment, though Lactantius certainly thought it was a cross with its top bent over so as to make the chi-rho monogram (the first two letters of the Greek word for 'Christ').

Against most expectations, Maxentius decided to risk a battle outside the walls of Rome. Constantine seized the opportunity and attacked. Maxentius's troops were caught off balance, and were driven back over the Milvian Bridge into the city. Maxentius himself was still trying to retrieve the situation when the bridge collapsed and he was drowned in the river. The next day Constantine entered Rome, convinced that God had given him the victory.

Early in the following year, Constantine and Licinius met in Milan to plan their next moves against Maximin. Edicts granting toleration to Christians had already been issued. Maximin sensed that he was in peril, and tried to forestall the attack by invading Licinius's territories in northern Greece. Licinius marched against him, with the support of the supreme God as his rallying-cry. Maximin was defeated at the Battle of Heraclea, and died soon after. With his death the persecution ended, except for a belated repression under Licinius at a later date. For nearly twelve years Constantine and Licinius ruled in uneasy peace, but eventually the break came. Licinius saw that as he had used Christianity as a lever against Maximin, so Constantine could use it against him. He began repressive measures, but in 324 Constantine moved against him, and he was decisively beaten at Adrianople in Thrace. He fled across the Bosphorus, but was surrounded and captured. Constantine was supreme.

11

The legacy

With the defeats of Maxentius and Maximin in 311–312, there ended the period of the persecuted church. While some great names of this period were to survive into the next, the situation was radically different. Eusebius and Ossius, or Hosius, of Cordoba found themselves changed from leaders of an influential sect to the confidants of the emperor.

For the first time, the Christian churches had unashamed imperial patronage. Constantine put Christianity on an equal footing with all other cults.[1] Its sacred days were to be public holidays, and its officials gained prized exemption from taxation and compulsory public service.[2] While in public pronouncements Constantine might not be over-exuberant in his use of Christian language (there is no mention of Christianity on his triumphal arch at Rome), and even though he was still officially 'Pontifex Maximus' (chief priest of the state cult), he made it quite clear that he was a friend of the Christians, even if at times his attentions were decidedly ham-fisted.

From now on Christians could be great personages at court, and in Eusebius we have one of the first court bishops. In spite of his nauseating flattery of Constantine, Eusebius was fairly

[1] Specimens of the legislation in J. Stevenson, *A New Eusebius*, pp. 300–305, 333–334.
[2] With the Empire suffering desperate economic problems, taxation was a crippling burden; public officials were responsible for collecting taxes, and had to make up any deficit from their own funds. Laws had to be passed compelling all with a certain income to assume public office (*e.g.* as town councillors). Exemption from office was greatly prized, therefore, but seldom given!

The Arch of Constantine. Erected 312–315, the arch incorporates early, as well as contemporary, sculpture. The relief of the Battle of the Milvian Bridge is just above the small archway on the right.

restrained in the use he made of his privileges. Those who followed him, especially under Constantine's sons, were less scrupulous. Imperial power was called in to support various theological factions, and to crush opponents; imperial favour was sought in order to gain election to the best bishoprics. The ecclesiastical politician dates from the time of Constantine, for the bringing of church officials to the royal court never improved their spirituality.

With the churches now in the position of favoured institutions, there was an invasion of court ceremonial into church services. It had long been the custom to carry candles and incense before important government personages. God, as the supreme Potentate, would be given similar honours. Larger buildings would be erected, often with government grants. Pilgrimage to the Holy Land became the 'done thing', especially after the empress mother Helena had gone to Jerusalem, demanded that the bishop should show her all the places connected with the Bible, and had then proceeded to build churches on most of the sites! And the bishop who was a

173

great man at court could hardly be expected to revert to his former humble mode of dress and ceremonial when he presided at his church on Sunday. Only fifty years previously, bishops had condemned Paul of Samosata for his ostentation. Now they were following his example!

Then, with the pressure of public disapproval and persecution finally removed, adherence to the church was an attractive option. Many of the old Roman aristocracy, to be sure, still retained their allegiance to the old gods, but the new men were often sympathizers towards Christian beliefs or outright converts. People no longer decided to follow Christ despite the great cost; it could even be an advantage to be a Christian. The lowering of standards had been so gradual as to be imperceptible. Eusebius believed that the last great persecution had been sent as a judgment on the churches for their slackness and worldliness, even before they received imperial favour. But the last days of the persecuted churches compared favourably with the tolerated church under Constantine. The day of the 'churches of the martyrs' was gone. Those, like the Donatists of North Africa, who tried to perpetuate it, were to feel the heavy hand of imperial repression upon them.

But for all the favour he bestowed on Christianity, Constantine did not extirpate paganism. This was left to the Spaniard Theodosius, the last effective emperor of the Western Empire, who made Christianity the state religion, and decreed penalties for those who persisted in practising pagan rites. Under Constantine the church still remained merely the most privileged among many cults. Constantine contrived to advance cautiously in his commitment to Christianity, even deferring baptism until he lay dying, in case he should commit some terrible sin after receiving the forgiveness for his past life. He still remained the soldier-emperor, whose main method of dealing with intransigence was to send in the troops and exile the ringleaders. Although he had the best of intentions, his behaviour often fell well short of normative Christian standards.

The last persecutions also left painful legacies which were beyond the ability of Constantine, or of anyone else, to settle. Even while the persecution still raged in the East, the Christians of North Africa were taking sides, and on the death of the bishop of Carthage in 311 their internecine strife came out into the open. In Egypt the trouble with Melitius became tangled with the doctrinal errors of Arius, and resulted in a bitter conflict that was to involve all the Christian churches for nearly fifty years. Even the church in the capital city, Rome, was not to be untroubled. The leadership of this great church was too big a prize, and many battles were to be fought over who should be bishop. Similar strife occurred from time to time when the great bishoprics of Antioch, Alexandria or Constantinople were vacant, but before the fourth century was over, thoughtful pagans were to express horror as street battles raged and left piles of dead, while the clergy fought each other for the right to be pastor of the Roman church. Already, in Egypt and elsewhere, some thoughtful souls were wishing to opt out of the new empire-building which had come on the churches. Antony in Egypt would lead the flight to contemplate in the desert, while his fellow-Egyptian

The base of the Obelisk of Theodosius, in the hippodrome, Constantinople. In the centre of the top half of each of the two visible faces of the obelisk, the emperor and his family are shown. Theodosius established Christianity as the only official religion of the Roman Empire.

Rigfeart Church, Glendalough, Co. Wicklow (Eire). *c.* AD 600. Ninian's church at Whithorn, where he preached to the Picts, would have been similar to this.

Pachomius was soon to pioneer the religious community where people could live together under Christian discipline.[3]

The times of persecution meant that for a while little thought was given to the missionary work of the churches. The embattled spirit of the times left small room for concern for evangelizing. In the aftermath of persecution the immediate mission field was among the new adherents who were badly in need of instruction in Christian doctrine and living. But before the century was done, there would be many who consciously set out to spread the message of Christ beyond the Roman frontiers. In the middle of the century Ulfilas was to reduce the Gothic language to writing, and to evangelize the nation where he had once been a slave. Athanasius himself appointed the first bishop to the Ethiopians. On another extremity of the Empire, Ninian was to set up his centre at Whithorn in Scotland and preach to the Picts. But it is also sad to say that the same century would see court bishops denying the faith they professed by lives taken up with the worst intrigues. The doings of the 'Christian' mob at Alexandria

[3] See Glossary.

were still a standing reproach.[4] There was also a spread of superstition, so that the bones of a martyr would receive more reverence than Christ Himself. The hunting for relics was often of greater interest to people than the study of the Bible, and Christian living was no longer seen to be a requirement of Christian faith. Naturally there were those who loudly deplored such trends, and who castigated the new-style dandy clerics and the credulous and inconstant congregations. But those who dropped out of the ecclesiastical rat-race often distinguished themselves only by exhibitionist forms of piety (*e.g.* how many prayers or genuflections they could do in a day!).[5] The toleration that the Christians had gained would allow them not only to worship freely, but also to tear each other apart with official backing.[6]

It is pointless to speculate over what might have happened if Constantine had lost the Battle of the Milvian Bridge outside Rome. The driving force among the Christians, even allowing for their many imperfections, was strong enough to have obtained toleration before long. Christianity did not need imperial backing, as is shown by the fact that the churches survived the collapse of the Western Empires within a century of their having been freed from persecution. With all the faults, there was enough of the Spirit of Christ still among the church leaders and members to ensure that the organization would continue in spite of political upheaval.

Without doubt, the apostles would have been surprised to see the change from the congregation of the upper room to the crowded basilicas of the era of Constantine. They would have applauded the missionary effort which had carried the message of Jesus Christ even beyond the bounds of the Empire. They would, no doubt, have admired the steadfastness of the martyrs who were now venerated. The drift towards formalism might have worried them. Certainly the lowering of standards

[4] With the connivance of the bishop, they murdered prominent pagans and burned down pagan temples. When paganism no longer existed, they turned their anger against those who differed from them theologically.

[5] *E.g.* Simeon Stylites, who lived at the top of a forty-foot high pillar. Theodoret, a fifth-century writer, saw him do over 1500 genuflections, at which point he lost count! Simeon was a great tourist attraction!

[6] The best account of fourth-century Christianity in all its facets is in H. Leitzmann, *History of the Church*, volumes 3 and 4.

and the internal strife would have come in for condemnation. It would be hard to say where devotion ended and where unjustifiable superstition began. While the message had not been handed on without alteration, it had not been ruined beyond recognition. And as men and women confessed their faith in Christ at baptism, it was still the Christ of the Gospels whom they sought to follow.

Index

Numbers in italics refer to illustrations; those in bold type refer to the Glossary.

206